Getting Happy

…when you wish you were dead

Conrad Hall

Praise for
Getting Happy
...when you wish you were dead

I am excited that you are about to let Conrad Hall take you on this deeply moving journey to getting happy.
— Jack Canfield, Coauthor of the *Chicken Soup for the Soul®* series and *The Success Principles™: How to Get from Where You Are to Where You Want to Be*

Conrad's honesty, his willingness to be exposed, make Getting Happy...when you wish you were dead a must read for every parent and friend.
— David L. Hancock, Founder, Morgan James Publishing

More Praise for Conrad's Work

Just bought and read Writing E-Books for Fun & Profit. It made your brilliance shine through rather dramatically.
— J. J. Medney, Esq.

I think I can build a good site (do have a little bit of credibility going for me), but your book is a HUGE help. Every little detail is thought out and plays an important role, and should be considered in the design and building.

It is NOT to be skimmed over. If you do you're just short-changing yourself. For a guy like me who's more of a 'fly by the seat of my pants' operator it is INVALUABLE to make me stop and consider each part as I lay it out.

— Don Mahoney, Founder, American Writers and Artists

The book is astounding. It is written as if you were my personal coach and knew my personal business and income issues etc. I feel that now, I can begin anew and actually find success online. These words really do not adequately express my joy.

-- Gordon Bell, Author, *Tell 'Em That's MY Money You're Messing With*

The book is great. It's very well written and is first and foremost unpretentious which is paramount when dealing with a new innovation. I like the textbook feel to it and of course the step-by-step instructions that, while very useful, don't assume the reader is completely clueless.

-- Adrian Newman, Marketing Director, Lombardi Publishing

Dedication

To everyone who has helped, and to everyone who has hindered. Everyone had their private intentions. Fortunately, I am free to choose my response to what other people do. We have shaped the man I am together, and I love and accept myself. That empowers me to have gratitude for every person who has touched my life.

CONTENTS

Day 45 – Tuesday, 25 Dec

Day 46 – Wednesday, 26 Dec

Day 49 – Saturday, 29 Dec

Day 53 – Wednesday, 2 Jan

Day 55 – Friday, 4 Jan – Confused, Suicidal, Despair

Day 59 – Tuesday, 8 Jan – Stressed, Doubtful, Wanting to Quit

Day 60 – Wednesday, 9 Jan

Day 66 – Tuesday, 15 Jan – Angry, Frustrated, Impotent

Day 67 – Wednesday, 16 Jan – Fearful, Grateful and a little Hopeful

Day 71 – Sunday, 20 Jan – Peaceful, Thoughtful

Day 75 – Thursday, 24 Jan – Shocked and Amused

Day 79 – Monday, 28 Jan – Saddened AND Energized

Day 80 – Tuesday, 29 Jan – Exultant and Encouraged

Day 81 – Wednesday, 30 Jan – Disappointed, Hurt, Angry, Betrayed

Day 82 – Thursday, 31 Jan – Disappointed and Misunderstood

Day 84 – Saturday, 2 Feb – Satisfied, Slightly Timid, and Sad

Day 86 – Monday, 4 Feb – Encouraged and Lucky

Day 88 – Wednesday, 6 Feb – Hurt, Angry and Depressed

Day 90 – Friday, 8 Feb – Intrigued and Validated

Day 92 – Sunday, 10 Feb – Sad, Wanting to Quit

Day 96 – Thursday, 14 Feb – Depressed, Resigned, and a bit Suicidal

Day 97 – Friday, 15 Feb – Chagrined and Disappointed

Day 98 – Tuesday, 16 Feb

Day 101 – Tuesday, 19 Feb – Belittled, Angry and Hateful

Day 110 - Thursday, 28 Feb

Day 115 – Tuesday, 5 Mar – Free, Happy and a little Concerned

Day 117 – Thursday, 7 Mar – Defeated but Resolute

Day 122 – Tuesday, 12 Mar – Defeated and Alone

Day 124 – Thursday, 14 Mar – Disappointed but Determined

Day 127 – Sunday, 17 Mar – Distracted, Re-Committed

Day 129 – Tuesday, 19 Mar – Frustrated

Day 130 – Wednesday, 20 Mar – Satisfied, Happy, Ambitious

Day 132 – Friday, 22 Mar – Productive and Challenged

Day 133 – Saturday, 23 Mar – Excited and Fearful

Day 136 – Tuesday, 26 Mar – Amazed, Grateful and Happy

Day 139 – Friday, 29 Mar – Excited, Satisfied, Drained

Read Me First

My first five books were written and published in 19 months. This book has taken nine years from first draft to publication. That's because this book tells my story.

I'm told the story packs a huge emotional punch. Naturally I'm no fit judge since writing the story has certainly been an emotional roller coaster. My hope is that laying this story bare helps parents be better and children be more resilient.

There are no apologies in this book, but the names have been changed to protect the privacy of others. After all, the important part is how I chose to respond rather than who did what to whom.

You'll find the opening chapters have no emotional descriptors. Those come into the manuscript about halfway through. That's how the journal entries appear. The only explanation I have is that it took me a while to recover enough that I could start to identify what I was feeling. Page numbers are omitted deliberately.

When you read this story, no matter how dark it feels, please remember the core message is I survived. You can survive, too. Find someone with whom you can connect – even if it's a fictional character. And try to focus on the things you get done each day so you feel effective.

Conrad Hall
August 2021

Foreword

The story you're about to read is compelling. Perhaps that is because it is also true.

Getting Happy ...when you wish you were dead tells Conrad Hall's life story in the context of a personal tragedy. It is the story of a man losing two families. In his early history, Conrad loses the family into which he was born because he was unexpected and unwanted. In his recent history, he loses the family into which he married hoping to replace what he once lost.

Conrad shines a light into the darkness felt by those who feel disconnected and ineffective as he weaves both stories together in the space of 143 days. When he finds himself disconnected from his new family, Conrad reconnects by learning to lean upon the charity of strangers. He builds back his sense of being effective by working on writing this very story; although it started out in a very different form from what you're about to read.

The story you are about to read took nine years for Conrad to write. The effort of working through the loss of two families, combined with the hard work of coming to terms with himself, turned the writing of this story into a process of deep healing and growth.

It is definitely a terrible thing to grow up without the love of your parents. And no matter how much healing you do, there is always an emotional experience missing from your life. It's no secret that the love and support of family is a huge boost to building a strong, positive self-image. And growing up without that love and support makes building a strong, positive self-image harder, but as you'll see from reading Conrad's story, it is far from impossible.

Getting Happy ...when you wish you were dead shows us that even the darkest journey, as a child or an adult, can be within our control. Your level of functioning effectiveness might be as low as simply getting out of bed and accepting meals from others, and your greatest connection in a day might be a briefly uplifting conversation with a cashier. Yet it is you making those choices, rather than staying in bed and not reaching out that makes the difference. It is you refusing to accept the circumstances you are experiencing and step by small step reaching instead for the life and the happiness you want to have.

This is what *Getting Happy ...when you wish you were dead* is all about. Conrad's insistence that the life and happiness he sees other people enjoying can be his, too, despite feeling such pain of rejection that many times death seemed the only way to stop that pain. It is the simple act of choosing to believe at a deep soul level that you are just as worthwhile and valuable as everyone else in the world. Ultimately. it all comes down to choice. You can choose to focus on being a victim, or you can choose to focus on making yourself happy.

After I read the manuscript for this book, Conrad shared with me that he made two rounds of edits deliberately aimed at removing all the language of blaming from his story. He knows that blaming temporarily feels good. It seems to absolve us of any responsibility. But he also knows it pulls your focus to what other people did in the past instead of keeping you centered on what you can do to forgive, release, and act to become whole again in the present.

I was delighted to learn that, inspired by the *Chicken Soup for the Soul*® series, Conrad is planning to develop a series of books called the *Getting Happy* series. His intention is to write a series of books that helps people successfully navigate through their life events so they can consistently make their way toward getting and staying happy.

As you are about to discover in this very compelling first book in this series, if there's one thing Conrad knows, it's how to weather a storm and come through intact even if a little tattered. May his story give you the inspiration, guidance and courage to never give up and come through your own, knowing that happiness really is attainable.

I am excited that you are about to let Conrad Hall take you on this deeply moving journey to getting happy.

Enjoy the ride!

— Jack Canfield, Coauthor of the *Chicken Soup for the Soul*® series and *The Success Principles*™: *How to Get from Where You Are to Where You Want to Be*

Today is my first day in an apartment. It's a victory, and the pleasure is so intense I feel physically stronger. My spine is straighter and my smile is real for the first time in months.

Life hasn't suddenly become some sort of garden path, but I know my trajectory has changed. It's no longer a downward slide. This isn't the first time I've been homeless and bounced back (it's my fifth, longest and worst) so I know bad things can always happen. I'll take the happiness that has come my way, enjoy it, and be prepared to face each day as it comes.

Squeezing the keys in my left hand… Standing in my living room… Looking at the "roof over my head," I turn toward the door of my new apartment. I close the door. Open it, and close it again. I lock it, and unlock it. It snaps firmly into place and has a satisfying click when opened. Lock it again, then unlock and open the door. I'm getting used to the idea of it being mine.

Turning left, I walk from the dining room into the kitchen just to look at it. Coming out of the kitchen, a right turn and short walk along the hall takes me to the bathroom on the right. Another step and I'm in the living room. The door to my bedroom is at my right hand. On the left, between the living and dining rooms is a walk-in closet so big it has two doors; one in the short hallway and the other in the dining room.

It's a small, elegant apartment in an old building. In fact, it's upstairs from the oldest funeral home in town. I'm glad it's a quiet building.

Then my mind starts to wander. I remember how I got here, and it's mixed with memories of childhood, being an adult, succeeding and failing, being hurt and sometimes hurting others. It's like that old song "I never promised you a rose garden." Life is definitely a bowl of cherries – pits, stems, sweet and sour together.

Being born the third child in a family with two children, and having parents who never let you forget it, is a twisted way to start life. By the time I reached twenty-eight, I had experienced every major event available with two exceptions: giving birth (I have a daughter), and having a terminal illness.

Aunt Geri and Grandma Charters were dead. I'd been married and divorced, and had a child. I was killed in a car crash, had a direct, personal encounter with God, been bankrupt, homeless, joined and left the army (honorably), lived as a criminal and ran my own (honest) business. And I counted thirty-two suicide attempts in my first twenty-eight years.

It all washes over me as I stand in my new living room. From heartbeat to heartbeat, I feel my emotions shift across tears, smiles, anger, awe, dismay, ambition, and more. I have to step across the room and open a window so I can get a breath.

It's time. As surely as I'm alive, standing here looking out onto Washington St., I know the time has come. The book – this book – has to be written. In 143 days, I've gone from having my greatest success - $264,000 in first year billings – to being divorced, homeless, jailed and back up to having friends and an apartment. It has been like re-living my life on fast forward. So that's how I'm telling the story.

143 days from happy to despair and back to getting happy; wishing I was dead along the way. And for those who care – fair warning: I have little love for religion, and a deep faith in God. I'm a hard man living with the motto Cranium Ex Rectum™ (literally, head out of arse), who is filled with the love and compassion that only comes from living a hard won life.

This story ain't pretty, it's as true and honest as I can make it, and it's mixed with hope and despair, failures and victories. Come share it with me – the journey from unwanted child to victorious man.

Day 1 – Sunday, 11 Nov

I came home a day early to share my success with Maria. I got up early, and drove straight home from Nashville, TN. Other than being long, I don't remember much about the drive.

The event in Tennessee was the Info Summit with Glazer Kennedy Insider Circle (GKIC). GKIC is a results and action oriented company that teaches business owners about direct response marketing. The Info Summit focuses on information marketing and marketing systems. It's an ideal environment for a direct response copywriter like me, and my status is raised by having had Dan Kennedy as one of my first marketing and copywriting mentors.

The success I had at Info Summit was signing six new clients. It meant $264,000 in first year billings, and a percentage of sales created in the following years. Six clients is a full year's roster in my business. This was the success Maria and I had been working toward so I was happy to leave early and get home to my wife.

When I got home, Maria wasn't there.

"Hey, Skyler. Where's Mom?"

"Oh, she's out at a party," Skyler answered casually. Skyler was Maria's middle child and daughter. Brian Jr. was the oldest, and Skyler the youngest daughter.

"Did she say when she's going to be home?"

"No, not really, but it's usually after midnight. Why?" she asked.

Choosing to ignore the mostly reflex question, I asked "Did she say where the party is?"

Skyler's attitude was casual until now. Suddenly there was that caution kids have when they know something they're not supposed to tell, and they especially know you won't like it.

"Well, she just said it was with friends. I don't really know where it is."

"Aha. I see," I said with emotions crowding in. "Okay, Skyler. Thank you."

"You could try calling her if you want. I think she has her cell phone with her," Skyler said with the urgency of wanting to fix a mistake.

"That's okay. I'll just talk to her when she gets home or in the morning."

It's impossible to describe how thoroughly crushed and excluded I felt. Maria and I had a Facetime chat the night before, and she said nothing about going to a party.

That was when I realized Maria, my wife, had built a life that didn't include me. The pain was just like being a kid again, knowing my parents were shipping me off for the summer.

~

My father was an only child. His mother wanted lots of kids, but his birth was difficult. I'm told she took her disappointment out on my dad, and I know he never got past that.

I was the perfect opportunity for him to vent his spleen for all his mother had done to him. As my mother once explained it, they decided to have two children. (My sister and brother were so well planned; their birthdays are three years and five days apart.) Then I came along three years and four months later – unexpected, unplanned, and unwanted.

It was after I started school that my parents started giving me a special vacation. I'm a December kid so I started school at age four.

I got to go stay with Aunt Bessie and Cowboy for the first half of the summer, and the Sager's for the second half of the summer. These were folks who lived across town, and they were friends of the family. I remember being in love with Mrs. Sager, and asking her to wait for me to grow up so I could marry her.

Life was good. Aunt Bessie and Mrs. Sager each gave me a lot of attention, and Cowboy used to let me watch wrestling with him.

Aunt Bessie and Cowboy were an older, retired couple who had a bird; a cockatiel. You had to be careful about opening the door because he only went into his cage at night for sleeping. He was always out during the day. Usually he'd stand on top of the fridge, or perch on Cowboy's hat (but only when he was wearing it).

The Sager's didn't have a bird. They had a swimming pool, and two daughters. They were only four blocks away from Aunt Bessie and Cowboy, but it was a whole different world.

Aunt Bessie was really big into crafts and sewing. Cowboy had even built her a small cottage in the backyard so she could have all the space she wanted for working on projects. One day when I was seven, she showed me how to lay out a pattern, cut material, and thread a sewing machine. It was great fun because someone was paying attention to me, and I was being allowed to actually do stuff.

After a couple of days learning, Aunt Bessie gave me a small project to do. It was making a star.

"Be sure to cut along the dotted lines, Dear. You need that extra bit of material for sewing."

"Okay. I got it," I answered as I focused on the cutting. It was important that I cut everything just right. It was my first project, doing it all by myself, and I wanted to follow every instruction.

Every corner - especially the inside ones - was snipped perfectly. Aunt Bessie even had special scissors for cutting small details like inside corners.

"I'm done!" I shouted. "I have it all cut. Both pieces. Can I pin it now?"

"Let me just double check." Aunt Bessie looked over the whole job. She paid careful attention to the inside corners.

"This is very good. You did a great job, Conrad.

"Go ahead and unpin the pattern. Then you can pin the material for sewing."

By the time the whole project was done, I was on cloud nine. I couldn't wait to tell my Mom about everything I had done.

"Aunt Bessie, can I call my Mom and tell her about the star?"

"Not right now, Dear. It's almost supper time. Maybe we'll call her after supper."

Aunt Bessie managed to put me off that whole evening, but I was right back to asking the next day.

It was "Aunt Bessie, can I call Mom to tell her about the star?" every couple of hours. Aunt Bessie finally gave in and let me call.

The phone rang until the answering machine picked up. It was my mom's voice telling me my family was away on vacation.

I hung up the phone.

The most valuable asset any person can have is the love of their parents. The confidence and sense of belonging that love gives is irreplaceable. I have been decades learning how to patch over what can never be replaced.

~

That's the pain that came flooding in as I realized my wife was living a separate life. She waited until I was away at a conference, then went to parties without me. When I was at home, she would announce she was going out. Whenever I asked what she was doing, she'd say she was running errands. She'd be gone for hours and come back with only a bag or two of stuff.

Occasionally, I'd ask to go along. She never said no, but when I was with her we'd only be out for as long as it took to shop and drive home.

This was the break we had been waiting for – that I finally put it all together and landed clients. I wanted so much to share it with her, and to celebrate with my wife.

Day 2 – Monday 12 Nov

A good night's sleep often brings renewed confidence, doesn't it? You go to bed worried or tense, and things look brighter come the morning. So I decided to try telling Maria about achieving the success we had been working for.

Our third anniversary was a day away, and we both had legitimate financial concerns. Signing six clients at the conference in Tennessee meant more than a quarter million dollars in first year billings, and an end to the financial worries. We could finally start focusing on our marriage and building us into a family. Maybe I should share a little history so you know where things stood.

Maria and I knew getting married was a tough proposition, but we had our reasons (in addition to loving each other).

In a quiet, serious voice she said "Why do you want to marry me? I'm 44, a widow, I have three kids."

I rolled my head to the side and answered "Those are my reasons for marrying you."

We were lying beside each other so I rolled onto my side to see her better. Holding her hands to my chest I explained "You're 44. I'm 43. We've both seen enough of life to know what we want. Yes?" She nodded.

"You're a kind, caring, loving woman who also happens to be incredibly hot," I said smiling, then teased, "And you happen to have the good taste to think I'm attractive even though I'm 43, divorced, at least twenty pounds overweight, have thinning hair, and apparently I fart like a brass band when sleeping." We laughed, kissed and shared a long, warm hug.

I leaned back and kept talking. "Maria, seriously... You say you have three kids like it's a bad thing, but I see three pre-teen kids. They're past the stage of being babies and toddlers, so we can talk and have conversations - the hard part of dealing with children who can't communicate is done. And you know my history... I never really had a family. You and three kids are the family I never had.

"As for being a widow, I'd have a lot more reservations if you were divorced. Having a former spouse in the picture always makes things difficult," I said with the knowledge of one divorced, and who had dated a divorced woman.

Looking at her hands, she whispered, "But what if it doesn't work?"

"Neither of us knows what tomorrow is going to bring, right?"

"Right."

"But we both know we're going to have to work at this to make our marriage successful." She nodded while still looking at our hands.

"We've already talked about this a couple of times, and I'm happy to talk it through as often as you want.

"We're going to need help; some kind of counseling. It's not even a year since your husband died, and we're looking at getting married. This is a permanent relocation for me from urban to rural and from Canada to the U.S. The kids have lost their father and now they have a new one. I don't think we can expect to handle all of this on our own, do you?"

"No, you're right. I'm okay, but the kids probably need someone to talk to, and it's a lot of change for you."

Looking back now, I realize no matter how old you are, there are times when we all make choices based on what we want to be true rather than what is true.

From my perspective it meant going from being single, living in a big city, and living the writer's life, to being married, having three pre-teen kids, living in a town of 12,000, and trying to fit writing into the bargain. My reason was getting that ready-made family. Growing up rejected by my family has given me a burning desire to have one.

From Maria's perspective (which I almost certainly do not wholly understand) it meant having a husband, a father to her children, and someone passionate about personal development to help nurture them. That was balanced with knowing that I would be going through a lot of culture shock, had little experience with being a father or husband, and that she had been a widow for less than a year. Her reason was getting the best for her kids. Maybe not so much in terms of me as a person, but in terms of my attitude toward achievement, self-development and integrity.

We were married November 13, 2009 – Friday the 13th – by a Justice of the Peace.

~

"What time do we have to be in the courthouse?" I asked as we got out of the car.

"One o'clock," Maria replied.

"Wow. We're earlier than I thought. That gives us more than an hour. What do you want to do?"

"Well, I thought we could go look at some rings. There's a jeweler across from the courthouse."

Astonished, I said "Really? You want a ring?"

Taking my hand, and smiling, she answered, "Of course I want a ring. I'm going to be your wife, aren't I?"

"Well, yea, but I thought you didn't want anyone to know. Everybody's going to know if you start wearing a ring."

"Oh, I won't wear it. I just want to have it for when I can wear it."

No honeymoon, and not even a party, because Maria wanted to keep the wedding a secret from the kids. Since Maria had been a widow for just fourteen months at that point, she felt it might be better for the kids to wait on telling them, and have a second wedding once they knew. We know it's a dumb idea now, but Maria was worried about how the kids would react, and I went along with it.

As it turned out, we didn't get rings either.

The store was quiet, and when the staff found out we were going across the street to be married, all four of them gathered to help us choose.

There were a couple of rings I ruled out because they were just too big for my hand. And I have to admit I was completely out of my depth. Jewelry looks good on women, but I've never thought of it for myself.

"Maria, I just don't know. Most of my life, I've been a carpenter. I always figured if I got married, the best I could do is wear a ring on a short chain. I'm writing full time now, so I can wear a ring, but I don't know what to pick."

"Just pick what you like. I'm happy to get whatever you want."

"Okay, but that's part of it. You're paying for the rings, I'm not, so I don't feel good about choosing," I said a little reluctantly.

I took a deep breath and said, "What I can say is that, except for the two that are just too big for my hand, I like each of the rings we've looked at. I feel completely out of my depth and very much want your help in making a choice. You know style, and colors, and dress much better than I do. I'm happy to be guided by your choice when it comes to rings."

That's when things really went sour.

While the four staff members were commenting on how sweet I was, Maria was clearly angry. As the lady helping us said "That's the most thoughtful thing I've ever heard," Maria said "I can't believe you won't choose a ring."

We both decided to leave the store rather quickly, and the day went from glad anticipation to "let's get this done."

So I go from being a single writer in North America's fourth largest city, to being married with three teens, and living in Tiny Town, U.S.A. You could say I experienced a bit of culture shock. It's not an excuse – just a fact – that I allowed the adjustment to stall my writing and business building. That's what brought financial pressure for us.

~

The morning started with me sleeping in a bit. The drive back from Tennessee had taken around thirteen hours, so I laid in for a while. It was nice listening to Maria in the shower, watching the sunlight shift, and petting Silas. He had also made the trip with me on his first outing as my service dog. Travelling is fun, but I dislike being entirely away from home. So I trained Silas as a service dog to keep a bit of home with me when travelling. (Unlike a pet or even therapy animal, a service dog can go everywhere I go; conference centers, hotels, restaurants, etc.)

When Maria was showered and dressed, I figured it was a good time to get up and talk with her about why I came home early. She was in the bathroom putting on makeup and fixing her hair, and I was excited to share the story of my success.

She looked good. Her black pants fit nicely over her curves, and she was wearing a multi-colored nurse's top. Maria had a nice collection of tops. They are the kind with a deep v-neck like hospital scrubs, short sleeves, and a chest pocket for pens and notes. Her boss is a cardiac surgeon and she very much — although unofficially — runs the office (and happens to look great doing an excellent job).

Hoisting myself up to sit on the bathroom counter near her, I said "The conference was great. Things really fell into place, and I have great news. That's why I came home a day early. I wanted to tell you about it, and get going."

"That's nice."

"Yes, it is. I signed six clients; that's a full roster. It means our money worries are settled, and we can definitely look at putting in the deck out back, and getting Brian Jr. a new bed.

"There will be some travelling, so I'm looking forward to having Silas with me. And now we can talk more about planning around the kids' schedules so they can travel with me sometimes, too."

Maria didn't seem impressed or happy. "I guess," she said. "I have to go to work."

She wound up the cord around the hair dryer and put it in the cupboard under the sink. Then she put away her makeup and headed toward the kitchen. She always filled up her travel mug with coffee before going to work. I just sat on the bathroom counter wondering why my great news seemed to be falling flat. Maria was halfway across the bedroom before I hopped off the counter to follow her.

"We can talk about it more when you get home, but I wanted you to know the good news before you leave. You know, that I've put things together, and

I'm making it work."

"That's fine. I know you'll do a great job, you don't need to tell me about it."

She sounded preoccupied, so I figured she had getting to work on her mind. We each had routines around getting ready for the day, and goofing up the routine pretty much always meant forgetting something along the way. So I toodled back into the bedroom to get Silas off the bed so I could make it before jumping into shower.

~

Maria was at the sink doing dishes when I came upstairs from my office. The house is open from the kitchen to the living room, so I leaned on the counter to talk with her. The girls, Skyler and Skyler, were watching TV, and Brian Jr. was in the loft playing video games.

"Hey. You have a good day?"

"It was alright," she replied. She was still wearing her work clothes, and looked tired. "How was your day?"

"Good, I got a lot done." I was thinking this would be a good way to fill Maria in on some of the details, and get her excited about the success.

"I started doing research on each of the new clients. You know, looking at their websites, seeing how they show up in Google Searches, stuff like that. And I used the afternoon to put their welcome packages together. I sent them a questionnaire by e-mail today, and then I send them the package at the end of this week. You know the box I showed you before with the DVD player, mug, candy and stuff inside?"

"Yes, I think so," she said as she rinsed off the dishes and put them in the rack. "I think I'm going to lie down for a while."

It was déjà vu. I had seen this kind of scene play out between my parents. It felt like a big magnet was pulling me into the floor. My feet wouldn't move, and I was too stunned to speak.

I didn't know it then, but our marriage was already over.

Day 3 – Tuesday, 13 Nov

The day dawned clear and warm for late fall. Silas and I were up early and out the door for a walk. One of many nice things about living on the outskirts of a rural town is being able to walk without worrying about cars; coyotes on occasion, but not a lot of cars.

When we got home, I gave him his food mixed with an egg. That kept his coat so shiny and sleek that Silas was always the center of attention. He is a black lab, and the egg makes his coat shine blue-black.

After taking care of Silas, I went to my basement office to get some work in before breakfast. With three kids and Maria having to get ready, I had developed the habit of staying out of the way while they used the bathrooms and had breakfast. I would come back up just as everyone was leaving to see them out the door.

This day was also our third wedding anniversary. Since Maria and I didn't seem to be clicking, I was wondering what to do about it. Part of an answer came to me when I went upstairs to have a shower and get breakfast.

There was a card on my bedside table when I sat on the bed. It was from Maria.

"As the journey continues I'm there with you." That's what she had written.

After being unable to interest her in my success, and discovering she was living a life without me, I was a little doubtful about the sentiment. That it was left with no hug, no kiss and no conversation left me wondering how to respond.

My mind flashes back to all the times Maria has said "I'll always tell you the truth. I just might not tell you the whole truth."

There was a time when she said this to the girls, Skyler and Skyler, and I stopped her because I was astonished. "Do you know what you're saying?"

Maria was surprised and perplexed. It never occurred to her that there was anything wrong with her approach.

I was probably too strenuous when I said "You've just told your kids they can't really trust you. Sure, you won't directly lie to them, but now they'll always wonder what you're leaving out."

She looked at her daughters and said gently, "They know I'd never do anything to hurt them."

"Really, Maria? How are any of us supposed to believe you?

"In the last three years, you have consistently worked to undermine all the work the kids and I do to make us a family. As soon as they draw close to me, you tell them just enough truth to draw them back to you. And you deliberately keep information back from me that could help me relate to them.

"How does that fit with you claiming to never do anything to hurt them?"

As the conversation plays again in my mind, I regret falling into the habits of criticizing, blaming and complaining. Maria reminds me so strongly of my parents; the half-truths, the manipulation of agreeing then not following through, the flat out denial of ever doing wrong. It's hard to keep the old feelings this dredges up from influencing how I behave with Maria and the kids.

The mind being the wonderful catch basin of memories that it is, that triggers a much older memory of change foiled by habit.

~

Mr. Franklin encouraged me to join the school play in grade 12. It was a classic musical called Oklahoma. He had been helping me to shed my anger and the violence that went with it. Other kids didn't talk to me – didn't even say hi – because they never knew whether I'd answer or just strike out with my fists.

Another fellow and I tried out for the lead; the part of Curly. They had us sing together, run lines, and sing solo. The teachers, Mr. Franklin and Mr. Blake, put on a very good show of pretending to audition both of us for the lead role.

You see, I know they were pretending because Mr. Franklin made it clear afterward. He said "You did a good job in the audition, but I had you picked for Jud Fry before we even started."

I was shocked and hurt, and even more worried by the prospect of playing the villain; a murderer and arsonist. "How can you want me to play that part? I'm just starting to let go of all the hate and anger, and now you want me to dive into a character filled with those things. That doesn't make sense."

"Oh, you'll be fine. Just don't let it get to you."

There was a lot of rage in me as I answered, "Listen, it was you who got me to try out for the play, you got me into the Bible study, and you even got me going to church. You know what I've been like. Why are you asking me to risk this?"

The conversation went on for a little while until Mr. Franklin gave me the ultimatum: If you want to be in the play, you're playing Jud Fry. I gave in because I wanted to act, but I also gave him a warning. I told him if anything went wrong, it would be his fault. And sure enough, there was one mistake.

I don't remember why it happened, but I do

remember taking a girl by the throat and pinning her to a cinder block wall. Of all the backstage noises, and the things we said to each other, the only sound I remember is the back of her head bouncing against the wall. I'll never forget that sound. It was the hollow plunk of a ripe melon only louder; like you hit it with a hammer.

I'll also never forget that Mr. Franklin put all the blame on me when he found out about it. There was no credit for my foresight, no apology for ignoring my warning or leaving me without support during the play. There was only blame, criticism, and complaint. It left a feeling of betrayal that only deepened when Mr. Franklin made a very public, tearful, Jimmy Swaggart style admission of adultery with the music director from the play a couple months later.

~

Memories like this replay in my mind as I wonder what to do. Is there hope for our marriage? Can a relationship last when one person insists on calling wrong things right?

My life's motto is Cranium Ex Rectum (literally: skull out of arse), and I'm wondering how to hold onto that while being married to a woman who prefers form over function. And I can't kid myself that this is a surprise. I certainly saw the signs before we were married. I even told Maria we would need counseling support to make the marriage work, and we both had reservations about getting married.

My warning to Mr. Franklin comes back to me. I knew playing Jud Fry was wrong. I knew Maria and I had hugely different approaches, and getting along would be difficult. But I set all the realities aside; just like in high school.

Day 8 – Sunday, 18 Nov

The day dawns bright and clear. Sunday is always a relaxed day with everyone sleeping in. Even I don't get up until six.

This morning, I was sitting at the kitchen table. It's a warm, oak finished table sitting in a bay window. The kitchen faces south so it catches the morning sun. My breakfast was finished, and I was holding Maria's card. I think about what has, and especially what hasn't, happened in the past week.

It has been a week of wondering what Maria meant with her card. She wants to be there as the journey continues, but we haven't talked all week.

There's a strange sense of being in limbo. I'm not sure how to start a conversation, so I just hang around hoping she'll talk to me. When she's doing dishes, I hang around the counter to watch.

"Do you want something?"

"No. I just thought we might talk."

"Oh, okay."

And she keeps washing dishes.

When we talked about getting married, we said we wanted a partnership; to be working together and making a family. It hasn't turned out that way.

"Would you like to tell me what this card means?" I hold up the card she gave me.

She seems slightly cross as she answers, "Just what it says."

I wait for her to say more, but she doesn't.

"Okay. It says 'As the journey continues, I'm there with you.'

"To be honest, I'm trying to figure out what that means when you haven't said a single word to me all week." She keeps washing dishes, and looks rather tense.

I started talking in what I hoped would be a calm, inviting manner. "Maria, I'm trying to understand how you see 'being there with me' when we don't talk, you don't want to hear about my success, and when I come into a room, you find a reason to leave. Can you see what I'm saying?"

Her voice burst out as though she had been holding back a lot of anger. "I don't know what you expect from me! The card says what it says. What more do you want?"

I didn't know what to say. The only thing I could think of was to ask "Why are you angry at me? I'm trying to understand what's going on. You give me a card that says you're there with me, but you're doing everything you can to stay away from me. I don't get it."

She didn't answer. She just finished the dishes then went down the hall to start laundry. I watched her until she had the first load of washing in the machine, then I decided it would be best to leave her alone. It seemed like a good time for Silas and me to go for our morning walk.

It's a mile to the end of the road, and Silas and I walk down and back every morning.

Silas is a great listener. He always lets me talk, and when I ask a question he comes over to me. I know it's just the change in my voice that brings him, but it still feels good to have him near.

As my mind drifts over the last three years, I know what I want to do. Criticizing needs to be replaced by caring, nagging gets swapped for supporting, and threatening has to be dropped in favor of negotiating. The behaviors I grew up with as a kid, and that we all see being used every day, are incredibly destructive. They're what we use to control instead of making the effort to connect.

But where is my limit? Before we got married we said we wanted a partnership. Then she asked for a prenuptial agreement that kept me from being a partner. Then it has been three years of seesawing. Maria asking for my help to build a family and urging the kids to follow my example – then sabotaging the progress we make to keep the kids close and me on the outside. Now comes silence after a card promising companionship.

There's no question we've both made mistakes along the way.

Where is the point at which you say "This is as far as I go. You are free to choose any behavior you want. But if you choose to keep going in the same direction, I can't travel with you anymore."

That's what happened when I finally decided to leave my parents out of my life. I was 34, and it was Christmas Eve.

~

That summer, my father and I had gone into business together. We were both carpenters, and I had grown up watching (sometimes helping) with his business of antique furniture refinishing and reproductions. He was getting older, was in poor health, and had asked me to help with his work.

I agreed. (No matter how lousy your parents are, there's always a part of you that wants their love and acceptance.)

I found us an inexpensive location for a shop in an old, commercial building next to a train station. It was cheap, had lots of room, and no neighbors to be bothered by the smells of stripper, glue and finishes. We had all his stock moved in a couple of days.

Then the excuses started.

I took short jobs through the summer while my father made excuses to not have me working on the furniture. I demolished a couple houses, and built some decks and fences. But by the time November was approaching, I was in a tight spot.

"Dad, what's going on with the furniture? There are almost eighty pieces in the shop, and I haven't touched one all summer. When are we going to start working together?"

He answered without looking at me, "Well, we can't do too many pieces at once. That would overload the auction."

"Okay," I said skeptically. "There's more than one auction house, I can take a load to flea markets on the weekends, and there's always the option to actually advertise what we're doing."

"Hmmm... I don't think so. I'm doing okay with what I have. I don't think I want to take on all that extra work."

I was angry at this point (anger has been a common response in my life). I could see the betrayal for what it was. I managed to keep my voice level as I made the situation completely clear for both of us.

"Okay. You asked me to come help you because you couldn't keep up. I've managed to keep up through the summer while you made excuses. Now we're headed into winter. There aren't a whole lot of decks and fences going in this time of year.

"I'm telling you flat out: If we aren't going to work together..." I took a deep breath. "If you aren't going to let me earn some money by doing some furniture, then I'm not sure I'll have enough money for November's rent on the shop."

His answer closed the last door.

"Alright. I'll make sure I have my stuff out before the rent is up."

I didn't answer. I didn't argue. I just collected my stuff, got in my van, and left.

With my mother in full support, my parents proceeded to take (or sell) everything I owned. As it worked out, it was Christmas Eve when I left the keys to the shop in the mailbox. I haven't seen my parents since.

~

That memory was strong in my mind as I walked with Silas. Maria's card seemed a lot like a lie I had heard before.

Our walk takes about forty-five minutes. By the time Silas and I got home, I had made my decision. I give Maria her card back.

She is back in bed when Silas and I got back. She

is awake and enjoying the opportunity to just lie in. I hand her the card and start talking.

"Maria, I'm not understanding this card.

"We've had our share of troubles, but I was expecting more reaction when I got home. I mean, having clients lined up means there's lots of money coming in and we can do some of the things we talked about. The deck out back, Brian Jr.'s bed, and time for us. But it seems like you don't even want to talk to me."

She put the card on her bedside table while I was talking, and watched me while I spoke. Then she got out from under the covers, stood, and walked around the bed to the bathroom.

"Maria, are we going to talk about this?"

She answers from the bathroom, "I don't know what you want me to do. If you don't believe me, then you don't believe me. I don't know what else to say."

I sit at the side of the bed wondering what to do. Experience has shown that trying to pursue the conversation is going to have bad results. Maria just clams up, and says she's too upset to talk. How do you negotiate, support or even care when the other person shuts you out. This is what we were trying to avoid when we talked about getting counseling and support in the beginning. Now that's a forbidden topic that only results in Maria saying there's no one local who accepts her insurance coverage.

Looking back, I think I could have hugged her, said something caring, done something to change our pattern. Instead, I gave up and went downstairs to my office. The place I retreated to like a rabbit diving into its den.

That night, Maria picked a fight in front of the kids over the dog being hers and she can do as she pleases.

Silas and I go for several walks every day. It's a great break for me, and Silas always enjoys being outside. This time, I was getting ready to take Silas for an after dark walk. I put a reflective vest on Silas, and then got my coat and a vest for me.

At the same time, Maria put on her coat and she and Skyler headed for the garage. Then Maria called Silas to her. I knew what was coming next.

When I got out to the garage, Maria had let Silas out to run free.

In a loud, accusing voice I asked, "Maria, what are you doing?" We had talked about this several times, and each time Maria had agreed to stop letting Silas run without a leash.

Quite nonchalantly, Maria answered, "I'm letting Silas run before we go for a ride."

"Yes, I can see that," I said evenly; clearly unhappy. "And I'm thinking of all the times we've talked about this, and you've agreed to stop doing this. So why are you doing it now?"

"He's my dog, and I'll do as I please."

"No, Maria, he isn't your dog. He's ours. I care for him, train him, feed him, and look after him, too."

"No he isn't. He's mine, just like the cars, the house, and the kids are mine. You don't tell me what to do in my own house."

I feel powerless, humiliated and betrayed. I toss the leash at her saying, "Here. You'll need this when he finally comes back." My voice is angry, bitter, and quiet as I walk back into the house.

The most frightening thing about suicide is that it, too, is a form of failure. It is the last line of a failing defense; an Alamo. The world has you outgunned and isolated. You can't win, and there's only one direction left to run.

You don't choose suicide because you want to die. You choose suicide because it's your last remaining hope for stopping the pain.

I remember walking along King Street in Welland planning how to die. There are a lot of options when you take the time to look around and think it through. Then I think about the times I've attempted suicide without succeeding. There have been close calls, trips to emergency, and even time in the hospital to heal, but I'm still here. More than anything, that's a testament to the power of our instinct for self-preservation.

It was never death I wanted. I simply wanted - want - people to stop being mean and cruel.

Day 10 – Tuesday, 20 Nov

One week since our anniversary. Two days since our last argument. Maria and I haven't said a word to each other.

I didn't go upstairs this morning when everyone was leaving.

The doorbell rang a little after nine am. Silas was downstairs with me, and I decided to run upstairs with him to see if it was a delivery of some kind. I didn't usually bother answering the doorbell during the day.

As Silas and I ran down the hallway and past the kitchen counter, I glanced out the kitchen windows. I stopped dead in my tracks. A sheriff's car was in the driveway.

Something inside me said this was bad news. For a minute, I actually considered locking the front door and going back downstairs. Then I realized that couldn't possibly bring good results, so I opened the door.

A Deputy Sheriff was standing on the step and asked, "Hi. I'm Deputy Sheriff James Beech. Are you Conrad Hall?"

"Yes."

"You're wife has filed for an order of protection,

and a petition for divorce. I have some paperwork here that I need to read to you, and then I need your signature. May I come in?"

It has always struck me as ludicrous that people pretend to give you an option when they clearly intend that you have no options.

I stepped clear of the door to let him in and angrily said, "I don't need you to read anything. Just tell me: Do I have to leave the house?" I was already furious and thinking poorly. I would, unfortunately, choose this pattern frequently in the months to come. Old habits are pernicious when ignored.

"Well, sir, I have to read this to you. Would you like to sit down?"

Of course I gave in, sat down, and listened. We all make bad decisions when we let our emotions run away with us, but I wasn't going to argue too hard with a gun-toting cop.

As the officer read through his paperwork, I was thinking about other things. I was enjoying being hurt and wronged because obviously I hadn't done anything to justify this, right? Maybe it seems strange that I was enjoying it, but it's the truth. Even though I was minutes away from being homeless, I was feeling vindicated because Maria had again chosen a path that avoided talking things through. (Letting anger run away with you usually leads to poor decision making.)

When Deputy Beech finished reading, I asked "So does this mean I have to leave the house?"

"Well, I just need you to sign this first," he said calmly.

"I'm not signing anything," I said sternly. I was angry, but I wasn't blaming this guy. "All I need to know is whether I have to leave the house."

"Yes, sir. You're welcome to pack your clothes and personal belongings, but you do have to leave the house."

"Fine," I said curtly, and walked away.

~

It was thirteen years ago. The door was closing again.

My parents had taken everything. I was living out of my van, and commuting between St. Catharines and Toronto to work as a carpenter in the film industry. I kept coming back to the shop my father and I had used knowing it was over, but desperately hoping to find a way of keeping the shop going.

I hadn't seen my parents since they cleared out the shop, but we talked on the phone occasionally. My mother wanted to know how I was doing.

Then came the week when the rent was finally running out on the shop. It was the week of Christmas. My mother called again.

I don't really remember what we said, but I remember the conversation. She wanted to know whether I had found a way to pay the rent for the shop. I told her I was working in Toronto and was making enough money, but I couldn't be in both places at once. The only way the shop would work was if Dad was willing to honor our agreement to work together.

She confirmed the answer to that was "No."

The last thing we did was make arrangements for them to pick up the key to the shop.

December 24, Christmas Eve, I left the key to the shop in the mailbox. I got in my van, left for Toronto, and haven't seen or spoken to my parents since.

~

I went to my office. Instead of thinking things through calmly so the situation could be handled well, I decided to send Maria a contemptuous e-mail. I actually thanked her for destroying my life, and choosing this path rather than taking time to talk things through with me.

Clearly, the last thing on my mind was that anything I was doing could possibly be confirming Maria in her thoughts and actions.

When I left the house, I took very little. I had my backpack with some current files and laptop, my wallet and cell phone, and the clothes I was wearing. I wasn't planning anything. I was utterly despondent. The one thing I kept saying to Deputy Beech was "It's finished. If she wants it all, she can have it."

So I left the house and started walking down the road toward town. I didn't even know where I was going.

Deputy Beech drove up behind me a couple of minutes later. He rolled down his window.

"Would you like a ride into town?"

I thought for a second and answered, "Sure. Why not."

There isn't a lot of leg room in the back seat of a cop car.

"Can I drop you off somewhere?"

"No," I answered with a big sigh. "I don't really have anywhere to go." After a pause, I said "Maybe just drop me off at the sheriff's office. You're probably headed there anyway, right?"

"Sure, I can drop you off there."

After a little bit of silence, he asked "How long have you and Maria been married?"

"Three years."

"How did you meet?"

This seems like a strange conversation when I look back on it, but I didn't give it any thought then.

"I came down here to work for a client. I had asked the cleaning lady if there was anything to do in town, and she suggested asking another lady named Nancy.

"Well, Nancy happens to walk around the corner right at that moment, so I asked. It turns out she works part-time at a wine shop, and they have a single's night.

"I told her that wasn't my scene. I was only supposed to be in town for five months. The she says 'Oh, that's okay. We get lots of couples coming to the single's night.'

"So I laugh and say 'That's really not my scene.'

"Anyway, I ended up at the single's night, and Maria was there. We didn't talk or anything, but we definitely noticed each other.

"When she was leaving, I thought to myself 'If she turns around before getting to the door, I'll ask Nancy who she is. Sure enough, she stopped two steps short of the door and turned back to look at me.

"I ended up asking Nancy about her, and we got together.

"Why do you ask? Do you know her, too?

Everybody in town seems to know her, or be related to one of her patients." There were only a couple cardiac surgeons in town, and her boss was also head of the department at the hospital.

"I actually knew her husband better. Me and his dad used to work together, so I've known Maria for years."

The conversation dried up at that point. I got very uncomfortable with the idea of an old family friend - who also happens to be a deputy sheriff - being the one to drop this bomb. Understanding was starting to dawn for how Maria could have gotten an order of protection when there was no history of violence, or even police involvement, between us.

After Deputy Beech dropped me off, I just started walking south; out of town.

Day 11 – Wednesday, 21 Nov

It was a long night.

Walking is not a fast way to travel, and I didn't get far out of town before night fell. I decided not to hitchhike. If somebody stopped, okay, but I wasn't interested in having to talk to anyone.

It was cold. November in northern Illinois is not a good time to be outdoors through the night. The wind had picked up, and I was feeling tired. It had passed eleven.

A farm came up on my right, and I decided to see if there was somewhere to sleep for the night. Only one light was on in an upstairs window. It was small like a bathroom window, so I decided not to knock on the door.

There were a couple of transport trailers and two barns in the yard. The trailers and one barn were shut tight. The other barn stood wide open.

It had metal walls and an open concrete floor. There was no place to sleep. But I did find a garbage bin filled with paper sacks. They were the big, forty pound type of sack. I gathered up half a dozen and headed out to the side yard where I had seen a blue spruce.

Sleeping under a tree isn't any warmer than

being out in the open, but spruces give a lot of cover from rain and snow. I put down a pad of sacks to lie on, then I crawled in with my head toward the trunk. My backpack had the laptop and files in it. That became my pillow. The two remaining sacks became my blanket.

It wasn't even close to comfortable. I managed less than two hours of fitful sleeping before I decided to give up. I crawled out from under the tree leaving the sacks behind. What to do next?

I thought about a suicide attempt that landed me in the hospital for several days.

~

It was in January, and I was in high school. I had taken up cross country running, and decided to put it to good use. It was snowing and after dark when I decided to go for a run.

I ran for about seven miles (far enough to be tired), then headed for Birch Court. A friend from high school lived on that street. My thought was that someone who knew me would find me in the morning.

It made sense to fall and roll a couple of times before getting to my friend's house. In my mind, that would show anyone who looked that I had run too far and worn myself out. When I got to my friend's house, I fell down and lay in the snow covered street until I fell asleep.

Hypothermia and dehydration kept me in the hospital for three days.

~

It was thirty-two years later, and you could argue I had more reason for suicide now than I did then. But my mind was focused on getting through the night so a solution could be found. It's amazing how much is determined by our attitude at any given moment.

I had passed a horse barn on the way out of town. It was almost an hour's walk back, but I figured that might offer better options for sleeping.

Luck was with me when I got there because the door to the barn was unlocked. Unfortunately, there was no straw or hay in the loft, and every stall was occupied. The best I could do was a plastic lawn chair and a tarp. It kept me warm enough that I was able to get some broken sleep until just after five in the morning. Then I figured it would be better to leave than push my luck by being found in the barn.

I head back into town with a sudden, brilliant idea. Yea, real brilliant.

My new plan is to rent a car, drive as far south as I can, then cross the border into Mexico and wander in the barrens until I die or get a better idea. Isn't that a fantastic plan?

It didn't work out quite the way I had envisioned it. I got the car okay, even though it was the day before Thanksgiving. And I managed to drive all the way to Loredo, Texas.

There were a lot of stops along the way.

My usual routine is to drive straight through. Stops are based on needing gas. So gas, food, washroom, and stretching are normally worked into a single stop every six to eight hours. This time, there were stops before some bridges, after other bridges. You see, part of my plan was to just drive into a bridge. Most of them have those yellow barrels around the columns, but not all, and you don't have to drive straight into the columns to get the job done.

That's why there were extra stops. I'd see a bridge and start speeding up, then I'd think about what it means to give up. Giving up and killing myself means all the people who called me worthless get to be right. It means there's no chance to set the record straight, or prove anybody wrong. It certainly means the pain stops, but it also means the game is over. Do not pass Go, do not collect two hundred dollars.

Every time I stopped I got out and walked around. I yelled, screamed, swore, cursed, ranted at God, complained about how unfair everything was, and even pounded the hood of the car. Lucky for me

I didn't dent the thing. Basically I had two days of temper tantrums while driving to Loredo. Not my best moments.

It did, however, get better when I got to Loredo.

Day 13 – Friday, 23 Nov

The first thing I managed to do in Loredo, Texas was get lost in a rough part of town. Luckily, I attracted the attention of a border guard because I stopped at the side of a road.

"Hi sir. Are you okay?" He called from his SUV.

"Well, I'm okay, but I don't know where I am."

"Where are you trying to get to?"

"I don't really know. I just want to find a post office, but my phone says I'm nowhere near one." At that point, I had the bright idea of getting out of the car to cross the street. I figured it would be easier to have a conversation.

Well, it was certainly easier to talk, but we were also doing a good job of blocking traffic.

"Listen. I need help, but we're obviously blocking traffic. Would you mind terribly driving around the block and meeting me over there?" I said, pointing to a side road that seemed to have less traffic.

"Sure. Go ahead, and I'll meet you there."

We were facing in opposite directions, so the border guard had to drive all the way around the block to get back to me. I stopped the car, and jumped out to go talk with him again. He must have been just about convinced that I was a crazy tourist.

At that point, he really wasn't far off the truth.

He gave me directions, and helped me find the location in Google Maps on my phone. It was quite a distance away, but he told me it was in a much nicer part of town.

The reason I wanted a post office was to mail my phone, wallet and other personal possessions back to Maria. She had everything else; I figured she should have the rest of my stuff. I was still fixed on giving up, but things started to change when I turned the last corner to get to the post office.

Now, I'm not much for organised religion. I trust that God exists, and He is in control, but people do a lot of strange, contradictory things when it comes to religion. So when I turned that last corner and saw one honking big church behind the post office I jumped on the brakes and stopped in the middle of the street. Fortunately for me there was no car behind me.

I sat in the car, looking at the church, thinking WTF. It was the only building on the street, and the street was a dead end.

A quick check on Google Maps showed there were three post offices between where I had been and here. Over that day and the next I went to those post offices. None of them are next to a church, but I didn't know that yet. I only knew there were other post offices, and this was the last one before the edge of town. What would possess that border guard to send me all the way to the other side of town for a post office, right? That's what I was thinking.

It's Friday afternoon. For the first time since Tuesday morning, it occurs to me it's time to maybe start thinking about what I'm doing.

Day 15 – Sunday, 25 Nov

There are a lot of things you can do when you're in a town for the first time. Only one of them is thinking.

Some of the time was used exploring the east end of Loredo. My thought was to find a place where I could leave the car and wander off into the plains of Texas. It turns out the plains of Texas are used for cows with big friggin' horns, so they're all fenced on the east end of Loredo. You could ruin a car running into one those brutes.

A little bit of time was invested in walking around downtown Loredo near the Juarez Lincoln International Bridge. Loredo seems like a lovely place to spend a few days if you aren't driving a car you've virtually stolen from the rental company, getting divorced, thinking about suicide, close to broke, and being completely self-absorbed. It was Thanksgiving weekend, and the downtown was alive with shops, bazaars, restaurants, and people enjoying their time.

~

It was Thanksgiving weekend then, too. Beautiful weather, but chillier and a different city.

I was on a government exchange program for teenagers. You live in three different places around the country with the idea of seeing different cultures and having interesting experiences. The program runs for nine months, and my most interesting experience was never part of the program.

We were staying in a small town called Kemptville. It's a pretty place on the Rideau River about an hour south of Ottawa, Ontario. Thanksgiving weekend rolled around and I decided I wanted to go to Ottawa for the weekend.

Now, this government program puts twenty teenagers from across the country into one house. Boys and girls together, sharing bedrooms, and freighted with all the joys and miseries of being teenagers. We were a delightful little group of insecure, posturing kids away from home. Our one source of "stability" was the house supervisor.

We all arrived in September. By the time Thanksgiving arrived, I was ready to have some time away.

Roger, the house supervisor, was very much into the touchy-feely mindset of let's all get to know each other and ourselves. That was completely alien to me, and very uncomfortable. I had no idea how to handle it.

So when Roger announced we could do anything we wanted for Thanksgiving weekend, I immediately asked a couple of the other guys if they wanted to go to Ottawa for the weekend. They decided to stay in

Kemptville.

The bus dropped me off in Ottawa on Friday, and I found may way to a hostel. It was a cool place in the old city jail. Instead of rooms, you stayed in a cell with bunk beds. Washrooms were at the end of the cell block, and the kitchen was in the basement.

I picked my cell, left my backpack on a bunk, and went out to wander the city. I remember finding a rooftop plaza at a mall called The Rideau Center. It was chilly enough that the plaza was deserted.

I was 17. I'd grown up watching big, grand movies with lots of dancing and singing. Seeing people like Fred Astaire and Gene Kelly dance like it was a college sport. And here was an empty plaza with lots of benches around the outside edges. It was empty, I was alone, and it felt like an empty movie set.

I danced.

Alone and uninhibited. I heard the music in my head. I copied the moves of Fred Astaire, Gene Kelly and Danny Kaye. For a little while, I was free. Everything was possible.

Then I spotted someone watching me from an office window. They were just watching. They might even have enjoyed my private little performance. I don't know because they were too far away to see facial expression. Not that it would have mattered. It was an adult.

I went from free and uninhibited to judged and embarrassed. I tried to keep going for a little bit, but the music was gone. There was just me being self-conscious.

I wandered off the roof, strolled around the city, and eventually wound up back at the hostel. I remember showering, reading a book for several hours, then going to sleep. There was maybe a little disappointment, but it was a good day.

That evening I met Ernst Peter Ziegwald from Dragonvedge, Germany. He had already crossed the country several times, and was a few days away from returning to Germany. Being an outgoing fellow, he invited me to join him the next day for hiking in Gatineau Park.

We left early Saturday morning and came back Sunday afternoon. It was a great experience and one of the five best memories of my life.

We talked about a lot of things, camped out Saturday night, and had a great breakfast Sunday. But the thing that makes it one of the five best memories of my life is a piece of one conversation from Saturday afternoon.

Ernst Peter was a forest ranger in Germany, and he was talking about the wonderful stretches of forest he had seen. Then he asked whether I enjoyed the scenery.

It seemed like an odd question to me because only Aunt Geri and Grandma Charters ever asked if I enjoyed anything. So I told him what I thought he wanted to hear, "I get a lot of pleasure seeing other people enjoy the forest. I'm just happy to be along."

Ernst Peter's reaction was swift and strong. "That's too bad," he said. "You should enjoy it for yourself, because you like it instead of letting other people decide what makes you happy."

That was a big surprise for me. People in my life didn't generally care about me enjoying anything. Here was a complete stranger who seemed genuinely concerned for me.

It wasn't some kind of miracle cure, but our conversation planted the seed that it's okay for me to like something just because I like it. That's why it's one of the five best memories of my life.

There have been a lot of times – like being in Loredo, TX – when I've held that memory like a lifeline.

~

Being around all those happy people and families did increase my feeling isolated, and feeling like an outsider. But the positive parts were stronger. To me, there was hope and life in the air. The weather was warm enough for shorts, there was lots of laughter, and people were having a good time. So even though I didn't stay downtown very long, it did help to raise my spirits enough to really start thinking.

Of course, there were also some realities that only became apparent because I was in a border town.

After scouting the edges of town, and wandering the downtown area, almost all my time was used wandering the grounds of Loredo Community College. It's an open, spacious campus at a bend in the Rio Bravo in the southwest corner of Loredo. There is a beautiful mix of historic and modern buildings, and the campus was quiet because it was Thanksgiving weekend.

The only person I was talking to the whole time was me. You could say I was praying, and I tend to think of it that way, but you'd still have thought I was nuts if you saw me walking along having a chat with nobody around. I didn't even have one of those cell phone earbud things. Well, I had one, but I didn't put it in the phone. There wasn't anybody around the campus to see me anyway.

So for most of Thursday, all day Friday and Saturday, and Sunday morning, I wandered around Loredo, Texas, thinking about what I had done, and what I probably should be doing. And I was waiting to go back and talk to the pastor of the First Baptist

Church of Loredo.

"Good morning. How are you today?" The tone was bright and cheerful, but there was no real interest. The world would be a much happier place if people stopped asking questions they don't want answered.

"I'm fine, thank you for asking. I know it's Sunday morning, but is your pastor around and available?" My eyes were wandering over the entrance while I was asking.

"May I ask what it is you're looking for?"

"Oh, nothing in particular. I just wanted to chat before your service." Sunday is always the worst day to try talking with a pastor. Everybody else calls it their day of rest, but it's the busiest day of the week for preachers.

"Let me find Bill. He can help you find what you're looking for."

Not knowing who Bill was, I followed the lady down a hallway. We found Bill quickly, and she introduced us. Bill was (and probably still is) a middle-aged fellow, maybe five-seven, in his early fifties with a round middle and thinning hair. Your typical, successful, middle-aged guy.

"Hi, Bill. This gentleman was asking to have a chat with the pastor," she introduced. And with that task completed, she nodded and disappeared down the hallway with her smile in place.

"Hi. I'm Bill. What's your name?"

"Conrad. So you're the pastor, or are you the one who always knows where he is?"

"Well, actually, as luck would have it, we don't have a pastor right now. We're in the process of trying to find one.

"I'm the treasurer, and I'm filling in to run the office while we look for a pastor. That's why Sarah brought you to me. What can I do for you?"

"I was hoping to talk to a pastor. I could use some advice."

"Well, I don't know whether I can help, but I'm willing to listen. Would you like to tell me what's going on?"

You have to give Bill credit. He wasn't in a hurry, although there were probably a few things that needed his attention on a Sunday morning. And he seemed genuinely interested in listening. I wasn't hugely interested in talking to someone other than a pastor, but sometimes you just have to take what's in front of you.

"Okay. My wife just filed for divorce, and I drove down here non-stop from Chicago. I'm looking for answers and I don't know which way to turn."

To Bill's credit, he didn't show anywhere near as

much surprise as he must have been feeling. "Well, I'll tell you straight: That's a lot to talk about, and I don't have time right now. I do want to talk to you, but I have to look after things this morning. Would you be willing to sit in on a bible study, and then maybe join the service? I can make time to talk with you after the service if you can stay."

I had already waited three days, right? What was a couple more hours?

I went to the bible study, but didn't say a whole lot. I sat with Bill during the service, and did my best to not yawn. When it was over, our conversation was shorter than I expected.

"What are you going to do now?" The question took me a little by surprise. It almost seemed like Bill had forgotten why I was there, but I could tell he was quite serious.

"I don't know. That's why I wanted to talk to a pastor. I feel like I should try to work it out, but my wife has made it completely clear she isn't interested in talking. I don't know what to do."

"I think that's exactly what you should do," he said clearly. "Go home, try to work it out, and listen to what God has in mind for you."

That really wasn't what I had been hoping to hear. I didn't want to go back, I didn't want to work it out, and I didn't want to feel brushed off. But those were the things I was getting.

Bill and I talked for a while longer. We shared a little more about ourselves, and who we were. For example, he told me he was the chief financial officer for a major food services corporation. Strangely, that got me thinking about my writing and how it's odd the way people end up meeting each other.

Eventually, we said goodbye to each other, and I agreed to take the advice he had given. It was one o'clock in the afternoon when I pulled turned off North Bartlett Avenue onto East Del Mar Boulevard. I was on my way back to Illinois, but I was not happy about it.

The monologue lasted about four hours. It was the same screaming, swearing, steering wheel banging tirade that started the drive south. Just like the drive south, it was accompanied with a lot of telephone calls to Maria. She didn't answer, so I left messages. Fortunately, I didn't yell or swear at her when leaving the messages. Each message asked why we couldn't talk things through, gave her a lot of blame for having been dishonest with me, and admitted I had done things wrong and didn't know how to make them better. Pretty typical stuff for someone not quite ready to admit having done wrong, and definitely not wanting to be the only one to make the admission.

Day 17 - Tuesday, 27 Nov

5:12 pm. That's when I pulled off the highway into Springfield. Twenty-eight hours and twelve minutes after starting the journey. I may not have liked the answer, but I was determined to follow directions.

It also brought me back to the car rental place. I had no money to pay for the rental, but at least I wouldn't be on the hook for stealing the car. I dropped it off at the rental office and walked away.

My next stop was to find Pastor Stan Pear. He ran a bible study and Maria and I had attended a few times, and he was the only person I could think of who might be able to help.

Tuesday is a youth night at his church, so finding him was easy.

"Hi," I said addressing the first person I saw after entering. "Is Stan around and available?"

"Sure, he's in the office."

The place was well filled with teenagers talking, playing games, and working on computers. Most of them nodded or smiled at me as I passed on my way to the office. Stan's church was in the local Christian youth center in a historic building next to the Illinois and Michigan Canal. After thirty years as a manager at Caterpillar, Stan founded this church, became a life coach, and opened Alliance Counselling.

"Hi, Stan. You seem to be in the middle of a packed evening."

"Hi, Conrad. Yes, we get a pretty good turnout for youth events." He stood up from the desk to shake my hand. "What can I do for you?"

"I'm wondering what time you wrap up. I'd like to talk to you if you have time when you're done."

"Sure. We're done around nine, but you're welcome to stay and hang out if you want. The kids are always happy to see someone new."

"No, thanks. I'll just go for a walk and come back close to nine."

Things were wrapping up when I got back to the church. I helped Stan clean up a little, and we started talking.

"What's up? You look like you have something on your mind."

"Well, I do. I have a lot on my mind, and I'm not sure where to start."

Stan was quiet, and we kept cleaning while I found a place to start.

"I guess you know Maria filed for divorce."

"She mentioned you were having troubles, yes."

"Really?" That brought a lot of bitterness into my voice.

"She wouldn't talk to me at all, but she told you we were having troubles." That sort of broke the dam inside me. "And did she tell you she got an order of protection to kick me out of the house when she filed for divorce? Maybe you can tell me how, after months of me begging her to talk to me and work together to make a family, she manages to get an order of protection."

"No, I don't how the courts work, but I can talk to you about what's going on with you, if you want."

Stan is obviously good at being a life coach. It was almost like he was prepared for our conversation.

"I don't know what's going on with me. My wife has decided our marriage is over, I'm not from here, everybody knows her, nobody knows me, I have nowhere to go, and I don't know what to do. I do know that the one thing I want to do is kill myself. What's the point of going on, of even trying, when Maria has closed every door?"

That, of course, led to what I recognize as the fairly standard cover-my-arse, mental health conversation of "Hey, you have to promise me you won't do anything to hurt yourself."

Where did anyone ever come up with the idea

that this helps? People who talk about wanting to die are in the process of giving up, and want help. People who have given up, and then suicide, have stopped talking. Asking someone to promise not to hurt themselves is actually a threat, and everyone knows it.

If you promise, the person asking lets you stay free. Their butt is covered because they asked you to promise. If you refuse to promise, they call the authorities and have you committed.

You're feeling vulnerable and afraid. You reach out for help, and if you say the wrong thing you get arrested and incarcerated even though you have committed no crime. Whoever came up with the idea this approach is helpful?

So Stan and I ended up talking. He even took me out to dinner to keep on talking.

The solution we worked out was that his church allowed him to put people up in a hotel for two days. It was for people who, like me, were in desperate straits. I promised to not hurt myself, stay at the hotel, and we would talk about my options over the next two days.

It was, I suppose, a good plan. But the best laid schemes of mice and men often come to naught. (A Robert Burns quote if you're interested.)

Day 18 – Wednesday, 28 Nov

Today is the first time I'm arrested.

"Good morning. Batterdrum County Sheriff's Office."

"Hi. I'm wondering how I arrange to go to my house and pick up personal belongings. You see, there's an order of protection and it says I'm supposed to arrange this through the Sheriff's office."

"May I have your name, please?"

"Sure. It's Conrad Hall."

"And the name of the person with the order of protection?"

"Maria Sanchez."

"Okay Mr. Hall. I have it." There is a brief pause. "Mr. Hall, I'm going to send Deputy Beech to meet you. May I ask where you are?"

"Sure. I'm at the Motel 8, room 116."

"Deputy Beech is on his way, Mr. Hall. Would you mind going out front and waiting for him?"

"Okay. Thank you."

"You're welcome. Have a nice day."

You don't really think they'd say he's on his way

to arrest me, do you? Most people wouldn't wait around for the officer to arrive.

Deputy Beech is an older man, in his sixties. He stands about six foot four, and weighs at least three hundred pounds; most of it in his stomach. He's clean shaven, white hair, and a mostly pleasant demeanor. Suspecting nothing, I walked around to the driver's side when he arrived and leaned on the rear quarter panel of his cruiser.

"Conrad, why didn't you just do what I told you?" He asked as he got out of the car.

"What?"

"I told you to leave Maria alone. I told you not to call, don't text, don't send e-mails, and stay away from her, didn't I?" It wasn't a question, and he was clearly not happy.

"With all due respect, officer," I said putting emphasis on the title, "you can say anything you want. What's the problem?"

"You have an order of protection against you. You did everything I told you to not do, so I'm sorry but I have to arrest you?"

"WHAT!? That order clearly says to refrain from doing any of those things. It's in big, bold letters. It says nothing about being prohibited or forbidden from anything." I shot back hotly.

"It doesn't matter what it says. It might say "refrain" on the page, but we treat it as you being prohibited."

And just that easily, I was arrested.

Day 19 – Thursday, 29 Nov

Even though I was arrested around ten a.m., it turns out there wasn't time enough to get me before a judge yesterday. So I spent the night in jail.

"Hall."

"Yes?"

"Time for court." The officer was standing in the hallway outside the cell block.

All jails are different I suppose. In this one, each cell block has three cells with two bunks and a toilet. Then there is a common area with the hallway in front of the cells, a steel table with four attached seats, the toilet, a shower stall, television above the shower, and a telephone next to the entry door. I walked into the hallway outside the cell block to stand facing the officer.

"Turn around and face the wall."

He had a set of shackles in his hands. In case you've never seen a prison film, shackles are two sets of handcuffs. One set goes on your ankles, and one goes on your wrists. Both sets have about sixteen inches of chain, so you can move but not easily. Those two chains are then connected by a third chain. The only way you can walk is by holding your hands at your waist. Otherwise, the chain between your ankles is too tight to let you walk.

"Lift your left foot." The first shackle is put around my ankle.

"Lift your right foot." The second shackle clicks into place.

"Turn around." An easier thing to say than do at this point. The guard holds the other end of the shackles down low so I don't have to worry about tripping over the chain.

"Hold out your hands." First one shackle, then the other, is closed around my wrists.

"Is there a reason why I'm being treated like some kind of dangerous criminal?"

"It's standard procedure. We use these on everyone."

Off we go to the courtroom. There were three of us being arraigned at the same time. I don't remember anything about the men with me other than that they seemed to know what they were doing. I later learned that people in Batterdrum County who become involved with the police, tend to end up staying involved with the police; almost like a cottage industry.

The judge ended up setting bail at one hundred dollars. I wasn't especially happy but figured I'd be out of jail in an hour or so.

On the way back to the jail cells, I asked the guard "So how can this bail be paid? Does it have to be cash, or can it be by bank card?"

"You can use anything to pay it except a cheque. Credit card, debit card, cash are all okay."

"Cool. I have a credit card in my wallet. How do I get this done?" I was, understandably, a little excited about being able to get out of jail.

"Where's your wallet? He asked.

"With all my stuff in the locker they gave me."

"Oh. That presents a little bit of difficulty," he said with concern in his voice. He seemed genuinely bothered.

"Why? What's the problem?"

"Well... You can't have access to what's in your locker until you're released, and we can't get anything out of it for you."

It seems like an awful joke, I know; almost a Keystone Kops situation. I was free to go as soon as I posted one hundred dollars bail. All I needed was my wallet, but the rules genuinely prohibited me from having access to my wallet.

It was no joke that I remained in jail until December 10th because of those rules.

Day 19 - 30 - Thursday, 29 Nov to Monday, 10 Dec

There isn't anything particularly redeeming about being in jail. Actually, it's like just about everything else in life: You get value out of it when you make the effort to get value out of it.

It would be great to tell you that I used every minute for introspection, self-assessment, and personal development. Nice, but not even close to true.

Out of the twelve days in jail, I probably spent two thirds of it being angry. Sometimes I was angry at Maria, other times at myself, and frequently at a system that treats "refrain" as meaning "prohibited." But I did make one or two steps forward.

Being in jail is remarkably similar to being on exercise in the military, with the difference being that you have significantly less freedom (but more space) in the military. There are very few minutes during a military exercise when you are left idle to do as you please. That's pretty much the status quo in jail; do as you please.

A jail cell is only so big, and it feels smaller when you're sharing it with three or four other men. A foxhole, sentry post, or observation post is significantly smaller than any cell, and movement can be dangerous in a post. The toilet has no privacy, but at least it flushes and has toilet paper. Nix on both those conveniences in the field.

The strange thing is that the time weighed far more heavily in jail than it ever did in the military. There was always a purpose in the military. In jail, your only purpose is to serve time. Eventually, you realise it's in your best interest to invent a purpose.

You can play cards and read books. It doesn't take long to get tired of crazy eights and gin, so I relied on books. The one I relied on most was the bible. There's a lot of wisdom packed into the sixty-six books that make up the bible.

The book of Job got read several times. So did Psalms and Proverbs. Job has always struck me as odd because it comes awful close to portraying God as a sadist. I mean, why would God tell Lucifer to go torture the person most loyal toward God? When you take it a little less literally, it becomes a story about persevering through hard times. It's also a story about trusting that things we see as bad today can turn out to be useful tomorrow.

That was in my mind the second Sunday in jail. The TV was tuned to a preacher channel, and this fellow named Joel Osteen came on. Organised religion isn't my favorite to start with, and televangelists are generally the bottom of that pile.

But this fellow happened to be talking about exactly what I was thinking: that I'm moaning and groaning about how unfair life is instead of accepting responsibility for the choices I made that got me here, and that what seems particularly crappy today usually turns out to be important later.

Part of me was thinking I've already had enough crap in my life. Another part was thinking I may not be responsible for every bad thing that's happening right now, but I certainly made some bad choices along with everybody else involved. So maybe it's time to start dealing with me, and spend a little less time worrying about things other people do - which I can't really change or control anyway.

Day 30 – Monday, 10 Dec

"Hall. Time for court."

Again with being shackled and escorted to the courtroom. There are only two of us this time, and I also have a public defender this time. His name is William.

The process in the courtroom is swift this time. Because I wasn't able to pay the bail, William gets me released on my own recognizance. That's cool, although I'm still pretty miffed at having had to be in jail for twelve days just because no one would get my wallet.

"Hall. Time for you to go." It has been several hours since I came back from the courtroom. I never did find out why it took so long, but at least I'm free. As I'm changing back into my own clothes, one of the guards asked me about my plans.

"Do you have a place to stay?"

"No, I don't. I don't know what I'm going to do."

The guard handed me a pamphlet and explained the PADS program. "This is someplace you can stay. They'll give you supper, a place to sleep, and I think they give you breakfast, too. It's at a different church every night, so that pamphlet tells you where to go."

"Okay," I say with hesitation. Being homeless is

never fun. "It's better than sleeping outside, right?"

"That's probably a good way to look at it."

"Listen. This order of protection says I can arrange to go to the house to get clothes and stuff. Do I go to the Sheriff's office to arrange that?" The Sheriff's office is across the street from the courthouse and jail.

"Yep. Just walk in, explain what you need, and they'll help you set it up."

"Okay. Thanks. Is that it? Can I leave now?"

As easily as I was arrested, I was released. Free to walk the streets and do as I please. Naturally I went straight across the street to the Sheriff's office. I only had the clothes on my back, so I needed some clean stuff from home.

There was a female sergeant who called Maria to make arrangements. She got permission for me to go out to the house the following morning, and arranged for me to meet a deputy at the office so he could drive me out there and back again. That left me a couple of hours to find the church for PADS that night.

PADS (never did know what that stands for) is an overnight shelter program. Churches around town play host each night, and most of them are within a four block area. One is in the north end of town, and another is outside town to the south. They have to arrange transportation for that one.

They give you a pad to sleep on with sheets and a blanket. Supper, breakfast and a bag lunch are provided, and the volunteers are entirely friendly. The people at the different churches were a big support for me.

The program is at the church in the north end of town Sunday and Monday nights, so I had a bit of hike to get there.

"Hi. What's your name?" she asked pleasantly.

"Conrad."

She looked in a binder without finding my name. "Is this your first time at PADS?"

"Yes."

"Oh, okay. Well, there are few things we need to do for your first time. We'll get your name, a contact number if you have one, and we take your picture. That helps volunteers get to know who you are."

There are always two or three volunteers at each PADS facility, and they were all nice people. But having my picture taken, and a little card filled in, felt an awful lot like being in jail just then. I can't say I was particularly friendly or talkative that night. I even found a place away from everybody else to put my sleeping pad for the night.

~

Being homeless was less of a shock than you might suppose. You see, this was actually my fourth time being homeless.

The first time I was nineteen and had just left home. The parting was less than pleasant.

I had asked to use the car to go to band practice. (I was a piper in a Legion band.) My father refused, and a short argument ensued. I thought to end the argument by telling him "You are most worthless piece of human genetic material I've ever had the displeasure of laying my eyes on."

Clearly, reconciliation was the last thing on my mind.

When I was part way out the front door, I hear my father get out of his chair and come charging after me. This time, instead of giving in to the beating I dropped my bagpipe case, turned, and squared off to fight.

My father stopped in the doorway.

He growled "I'd go through you like shit on a hot tin roof."

I was afraid and just as angry as he was. "You're welcome to try Old Man," I said looking him straight in the eye.

That was my last day living with my parents. I was only homeless for a few hours. I asked a friend at band practice if I could stay with him until I got organised. That lasted a few months until I moved in with my future wife.

Of course, the next time I was homeless was when I got divorced from that future wife. This time, I really was homeless. I was 21. (Yes, it was a short marriage.)

It was about two weeks before I managed a bed in a Salvation Army men's shelter. I lived there for eight months before I got a room in a hotel. It was a nice, big room on the second floor. It was directly over the stage of the strip joint downstairs.

My next bout with being homeless came at age 34. This one lasted six years and had a lot of good things going for it.

I ended up homeless because my last effort at a relationship with my father cost me most of what I owned. My parents took what I had and I was left living in my van. I had my carpenter's tools, my van and my clothes.

The good parts are that I was working in film at the time. So it was easy for me to park my van wherever we were building sets at the time. Of course, nobody knew I was homeless at the time. I just told everyone it was easier to stay in my van during the week instead of driving an hour and a half to get home every day, and then drive back in the morning.

So, I was making good money, had a YMCA membership for showering and shaving, and wherever I was working had an ad hoc security guard at night. It was a little cold in winter, but I enjoyed the freedom.

Now, you might wonder why I would keep living in a van for six years. I've wondered the same thing now and again.

I think it was mostly a case of being fed up with trying to do things the way everybody says they should be done. I tried having a relationship with my parents and it got me bankrupt and homeless. Being married turned out to be a poor choice, and I just didn't see the point of spending money on an apartment for the sake of somewhere to sleep.

I got comfortable staying in my van. I was happy being free of the crap that goes with fitting in.

I didn't bother getting an apartment until after I got a girlfriend. She never knew I was homeless. I just told her my apartment was in another city, and I went home on weekends. When I got an apartment in Toronto, it was because we had decided to move in together.

Fast forward another six years, and we have my fourth time being homeless.

I had gone to the U.S. to work with a client and ended up meeting Maria. We got married. It lasted three years. Then we got divorced, and I was homeless again. This time, I was living in church basements in an Out of The Cold program; no van, no tools. I had a laptop and my vision for this book to keep me going.

Day 33 – Thursday, 13 Dec

The trip to the house for clothes went off without a hitch two days ago. Maria was out with Silas, and the kids were gone to school, so it was just me and the deputy in the house.

I filled a gym bag with shirts, socks and underwear. Picked up a book called Stop the Anger Now from my office, along with files for Generation E - a project I had been working on before all this happened.

The volunteers at PADS have been good about welcoming me to the program, and making sure I know how things work at each location. Last night was interesting because Wednesday is the night for the church that's way south of town. The transportation they arrange is in the Sheriff's van.

It pulls up to the courthouse at 5:30, and everyone piles in. If you miss it, you're on your own for getting out to the church. It's a fairly short ride, but I never did enjoy being inside a vehicle where I can't open the door.

A big development today was being officially declared a Poor Person.

Tomorrow is the deadline for responding to Maria's petition for a divorce, and there's a two hundred dollar fee for filing a reply. Since I didn't have that amount of money to spend, I had to apply for permission to file a reply as a Poor Person. That means they waive the fee.

Fortunately, the process was swift. A lady in the clerk's office gave me the form, I filled it in, and she passed it off to the court clerk right away. The answer came back the same day, and I even got a piece of paper with the court's seal on it saying they recognise me as a Poor Person. Not exactly a keeper for framing.

It reminds me of having to file for bankruptcy in my early twenties (my first divorce and second time being homeless). There is a class you're required to attend that's supposed to help you better understand money and how to handle it. The only thing I remember about that class is the fellow in charge being particularly mean about stressing how most of the people in the room were just irresponsible, and that they'd be back in the same class a few years later. He even said that most people who file for bankruptcy once become people with chronic debt and repeated bankruptcies.

Why is it that people who are supposed to be helping you make your life better so often take great pleasure in telling you how screwed up you are? I've met a lot of people throughout my life who claimed to want to help, who then focused on how big or terrible the problem is and all the reasons why I can't solve it.

Fortunately, it isn't often that I've met someone like the fellow running the bankruptcy class. It's true that you don't really matter to most of the people you meet when you're having a hard time, but you don't not matter to them either. Most folks want to be helpful, to ease your burden where they can, but nobody would ever have enough energy to get personally involved in every client's life, right?

The lady in the clerk's office was that sort of person. I wish even one conversation was in my journal so I could show you instead of telling, but I don't even have her name. There were several times when she answered questions I should have asked, but didn't even know the questions. She was courteous and helpful at the same time that she kept a professional distance. Does it make sense if I say the courtesy and the distance were equally appreciated?

Day 34 – Friday, 14 Dec

This is the day I lost the first of my clients. It was hard to write them about what is happening, but I have to be honest about my ability to perform. I'm depressed all the time and it's hard to keep my thoughts straight.

There's part of me that feels verified in losing the clients; even in having all of these negative things happen. That's scary. It isn't how anyone should feel, I know. There's a fatalism that builds up inside when you grow up with a lot of negative input. It's precisely like the line in Pretty Woman when Julia Roberts says "It's easier to believe the bad stuff."

The easiest thing to do is scream about it all not being fair, but life simply isn't fair. Having my Aunt Geri die before I was ready to lose her wasn't fair - it wasn't what I wanted - but that didn't keep it from happening. How fair is it to have parents who don't want you around?

Fortunately, taking concrete action usually takes your mind off whether something is fair, or even wrong, and gets you thinking about what you can do about the situation. Filing the form to be declared a poor person, filling in the forms to respond to Maria's petition for divorce, and learning the ropes at PADS were all concrete actions. I remember sitting in the library thinking about that on this day.

An e-mail came from that first lost client today.

He said it was too bad about what was happening, and it explained why I hadn't gotten things done.

The part about not having gotten things done doesn't sit well, but that's what has me thinking. I start looking at what I have gotten done in the last couple of weeks and what resources I have to keep working.

It's true that I can't effectively serve customers while homeless and going through a divorce. It's true that I'm homeless and have no income. It's also true that I still have my brain, my health, a place to stay each night, and can work at the library every day except Sunday. It isn't what I was planning for, or expecting, when I got home from Tennessee, but it's something to work with.

There was a project I launched on July 1st called Generation E. The vision for the project was to create the world's largest generation of entrepreneurs. The whole project can't go forward in my present circumstances, but part of it can. This book was part of that project, and I can still go forward with it.

Getting Happy... when you wish you were dead is my final healing step. It's the tool I use for finally setting to rest the loose ends, hateful memories, and POOPy habits (Personally Offensive and Obstructive) I've picked up along the way.

Even if no one else ever reads it, writing this book is my next step in the healing process.

Day 36 – Sunday, 16 Dec

My 46th birthday. I'm alone. No one knows it's my birthday, and I miss Maria. I still wonder why she chose to do this now. Did my success trigger something in her that doesn't want to prosper? Is she cheating, and this is a convenient out? Is there something wrong with me that makes it impossible for me to love someone, or be loved?

I feel like a failure. The one thing I want to achieve in life is to love a woman well, and I have failed. I try to be balanced – that relationships take two people and all that – but all I see is my own failure. I want to love and be loved.

The memory that comes to me is of Martina. A woman who loved me, and a woman I loved. I got it right for at least a little while.

Martina and I met while studying at the National Institute for Broadcasting. I had been doing improvisation at The Second City for a while, was doing some acting, and wanted to develop my voice talents. I was living in St. Catharines and working for the City as a seasonal parks employee.

When the summer season wrapped in the Parks Department, Martina and I decided I should move in with her in Toronto, and work at finding acting gigs. By the following spring, I had done a lot of training and gained experience but hadn't landed steady work. So Martina and I talked about my going back to St. Catharines and working for the city.

"The return notice came from the city this week." We had gone to St. Catharines to check my mail, and get out of the city for a while.

"What does that mean?" Martina asked.

"Well, if I go back, it means I need to be back in St. Catharines in a couple of weeks. So we need to decide whether I'm going to stay here or go back to work for the city."

"You're welcome to stay. I understand why you would want to go back and have a regular paycheck, but you don't have to."

"Thank you, Martina. That means a lot. But I'm afraid of becoming a burden to you. I already feel like I've gotten lazy, and I'm not pushing myself to find the work."

In the end, I chose to go back to St. Catharines. It was the safest path. One of the results was Martina and I drifting apart.

Our relationship wasn't perfect, but we were good together. I loved her, and still do. She loved me. So I know that I can do it, even if I only succeeded for a little while. That's something to build upon.

Day 37 – Monday, 17 Dec

"So, Conrad," Brian Walker said with a smile and welcoming gesture. "What can I do for you?"

Pastor Stan Pear also owned Alliance Counselling. He had arranged an appointment for me at the office in Palmerville (a twenty minute trip by car).

After filling in a few forms, Brian Walker walked me to a small office. We sat in not particularly comfortable chairs with Steve holding my now-official-patient file folder, and me slouching in my chair in an effort to be comfortable.

"So, what can I do for you, Conrad?"

"I'm not sure. That's a big question, so I'm not sure where to start and, to be honest, I don't know what you can or can't do," I answered bluntly. I was there, and willing to work, but not entirely happy with the situation. Besides, I didn't know this guy from Adam, and had no idea whether I would like him enough to trust him as a counsellor.

There was a slightly surprised look on his face as he answered "That's fair.

"Would you like to start by telling me what it is you want to do? Is there something you want to achieve?"

That seemed like a genuine question, so I sat up in my chair. Now that he had my attention, my attitude was significantly more engaged and intense.

"Okay. That I can answer.

"Maria, my wife, has obtained an order of protection and filed for divorce. I don't really expect we're going to work things out, but whether we do or not, I need to look at what has happened and the things I did."

I was already on a roll, and Steve was clearly paying attention, so I kept right on rolling after pausing slightly to give Steve a chance to say something.

"Okay. No relationship is fifty-fifty, and very few things are one hundred to zero either. So I see me needing to do two things: First, I need to figure out what I really am responsible for and how to do better next time around. And second, I need to get clear about the things I'm blaming Maria for - or anyone else in my life, for that matter - and stop blaming them.

"Now, I'm not saying Maria hasn't done anything wrong. We both made mistakes, and did things wrong. What I'm saying is that I know I can only take responsibility for things I can control; my own behavior. Blaming Maria, or anybody else, doesn't do me any good. Even if they did something wrong, blaming somebody is like waiting for them to do something about it instead of taking action for myself.

"Does that make sense?"

Steve nodded, saying "Yes. That makes complete sense." He hadn't made any notes yet, and he was listening actively, so I kept talking.

"Even if Maria and I never get back together, there's going to be a relationship with somebody at some point in my life. I want to know how to look at what I'm doing and decide whether it's right or not.

"And I don't mean 'Well, I'm right so you should do what I'm saying' sort of right. I did a lot of that with Maria, and it just didn't work. She pretty much always acknowledged that I was right, and even encouraged the kids to follow my example, but it never made any difference to how she behaved."

By this time I was really involved in hunting for the solution. I was sitting forward in my chair, my hands were gesturing, and I was excited that someone was actually listening to me.

"I know as much as anybody that it doesn't any good to be right if the other person isn't listening. That's my biggest problem: I know the right thing to do, and then expect other people to listen just because I'm right. I don't make time, or take time, or whatever it is I need to do, to help the other person go through the same learning curve I went through so they can get to the same place as me.

"That's what I want. I want to know what I'm really responsible for so I can do better, and I want to stop blaming people because that only gives them control over me.

"Does that answer what you were asking?" I asked as I sat back and waited for his reaction. He hardly paused at all before answering.

"Yes. That's very clear.

"You've obviously given this a lot of thought."

I jumped right in at that point, "You bet I have. Everybody I've met in the last few weeks keeps telling me I'm blaming Maria, I'm blaming Maria, I'm blaming Maria. Well, I'm not entirely sure I agree with that.

"You see, I think it's completely correct to expect other people to step up and acknowledge responsibility just like I'm doing, and just like everybody keeps harping on me to do. But here's the thing...

"Let's take my parents as an example. They did lots of things that parents shouldn't do. Okay?"

I waited to get a nod of understanding from Steve, then continued.

"Okay. So I look back over my childhood and say 'Alright Mom and Dad. It was wrong for you to ship me off to other people so you could take Faye and Joe - my brother and sister - on the family vacation.'

"Now here's what I think... It's fine, good, right, whatever for me to expect my parents to own up to having done something wrong. But that doesn't mean they're going to own up to it. That's the first part.

"The second part is: If I stop learning or developing because I'm waiting for them to take responsibility, then I'm wrong and I'm hurting myself. And if I say 'Well, I'm doing what I'm doing because my parents did this or that' then I'm actually giving away control of my life. Now, I don't want to do that.

"But here's the thing: I did that all the time with Maria. She would do something, I would choose my response, then I'd say 'I'm doing this because you did that.' Maybe I'm wrong, I don't know, but that seems an awful lot like saying I'm doing something today because my parents did a thing to me thirty years ago. Am I on the right track here, or what?"

I must have been talking like a fire hose, because Steve took a few seconds to think before answering.

"Well, I'll grant that they're not exactly the same, but yes, I'd say you're on the right track."

I nodded with satisfaction, and Steve looked like he was still thinking, so I waited to hear whatever he was thinking.

"Hang on a second. I have something you might want to work on."

He got up and left the room. I sat and waited. It was encouraging to me that someone was listening and appeared ready to help me take action. I didn't know this would be the last time Brian Walker and I would ever speak.

He came back into the office with some stapled sheets of paper in his hand.

"This is the Gottman 17 Areas Scale. It's usually used with couples who want to do what you're talking about, but I think it's a good place for you to start. You obviously won't be able to talk with your wife about the answers, but will you consider walking through the questions and answering them as best you can?" He asked as he handed me the pages.

"This might be a good way to work out what you're responsible for, and what Maria is responsible for, without getting into the blaming of 'I did this because she did that.'"

I was looking at the pages and reading the questions. "Okay. That sounds good. Wow, this covers a lot of ground.

"How long does it usually take to work out answers for all this stuff?"

"There's no time limit, and there's not really a right or wrong way to answer the questions," Steve answered as he sat down. "It's normally used as a discussion tool. In your case, what I suggest is answering what you can and then looking at the answer.

"Wherever you write something that says 'Maria did this so I did that,' then you can go back and rewrite it so you're taking responsibility for your actions.

"Instead of writing 'Maria did this so I did that,' you write 'Maria did this, and I chose to do that.'

"If you think what you did was wrong, or maybe you could have done something different, then you write that in too."

"Okay. Cool. I'm not sure what I'm doing yet, but I get the idea. I can do this."

We talked more about answering the questions, and what was happening in my life. We ended up talking for just over an hour until the fellow who had given me a ride knocked on the door and asked how much longer we would be.

As soon as I saw his face, I realised Steve and I must have been talking for quite a while. Steve was surprised by anyone knocking and interrupting, so I chimed in to explain.

"Ah, yes. It must be later than I thought.

"Steve, this is John. He's a pastor at one of the PADS congregations, and he gave me a ride here tonight." Then I shifted my attention to John.

"I apologise. I didn't realise we had been talking so long. We'll wrap up right now so you and I can get going."

"Okay. I'll just wait out here," John answered as he closed the office door.

"I guess that means we need to wrap up," Steve said. "Would you like to schedule another appointment?"

"Yes, I would, but getting here is a bit of an issue. I don't have a car, and the transit service requires me to done by six p.m. for me to get a ride back to Springfield. Do you have daytime appointments?"

"I do have daytime appointments on Saturday, but only evening times during the week. Will that work for you?"

"I'm not sure," I said while thinking it was not likely to work. "Let me talk with Pastor Cook. I have to take care of the co-pay anyway, so let me talk to him and see what we can work out. If we can arrange the transportation, then I'll book another appointment. Okay?"

"Works for me. It was good to meet you, Conrad."

That was the last time I saw, or even spoke to, Brian Walker. Since there was no way for me to keep paying the $20 co-pay for each visit, and I had no way of getting to the appointments, we didn't see each other again.

But I did keep the pages he had given me. I worked out long, detailed answers that helped me take personal responsibility, and even helped with writing this book.

Day 38 – Tuesday, 18 Dec

In the morning I am hopeful. There are two hearing scheduled for today.

One is for the supposed violation of an order of protection that clearly states I am to refrain from contacting Maria. The other is a hearing to determine whether the order of protection is to stay in place, and I am confident of it being withdrawn.

The first hearing starts at ten a.m. At first I wasn't sure it was going to happen. There is a process where the public defender calls out all the names of people he is seeing before court begins. My name was not called.

I went to the door of the public defender's office. "Excuse me."

"I'm busy right now with clients. I'll see you in the order your name was called."

"Well, that's why I'm here. I have a slip that says I'm supposed to be here today, but my name wasn't called."

That resulted in a check of the files, and a question put to the room about anyone else not having been called. It turned out the public defender's assistant had to run back to the office for three files.

When it was my turn to see the public defender I raised my question about the order of protection.

"How is it that I can even be arrested for violating an order that, in big, bold, black letters says I am to refrain from contacting Maria?"

"You won't get far with that line here. Is there anything else you want to ask before we go into court?"

"No."

The process in court was equally quick. The public defender, William Paternost, asked for the case to be postponed until January. The State's Attorney agreed, and a new date was set.

This is something that has always confused me. Refrain means to keep yourself from doing something. That's a long way from prohibited – you're not allowed to do it. It's sort of like farting in public. It's a good idea to refrain, but it's far from prhobited. And to top it off, even the state attorney said I reached out to Maria to tell her I lover her and ask to work things out.

The morning's excitement was over.

The second hearing started at two p.m. I was surprised that it was the same judge as during the morning, but I didn't think it would matter. Maria gave her testimony first.

"Your Honor, he yells and swears when he gets angry, and I have a photo of where he put a hole in the bedroom wall once when he was angry.

"He also once hit my daughter Skyler in the head."

I don't know correct court protocol, but I interrupted at that.

"Excuse me?! I have never struck you or the kids."

"Mr. Hall," the judge intoned. "Please don't interrupt. You'll have your turn."

Maria chose to reply to what I said.

"Skyler told me there was something about her closet door, and you hit her in the head."

The memory immediately leaped to mind, and I replied. "Okay. Except that isn't quite true. Yes, I did make a light flick at her hair, but I certainly didn't hit her. And why are testifying about something you weren't there to see?"

The judge took part at this point.

"Ms. Sanchez, was your daughter injured in any way?"

"No."

"And do you have any proof that this incident happened?"

"No."

"Okay. And do you have any other testimony to offer?"

"No sir. I'm finished."

"Thank you. Mr. Hall, you may offer testimony."

"Thank you, your Honor. May ask her questions?"

"Certainly."

"Thank you. Maria, before you and I were married, did we talk about my having a problem with anger and needing to get help?"

"Yes."

"And did we also talk about all of us needing help for us to become a family? That Brian had recently died, so you and the kids would need help, and I was coming from a completely different background so I would need help?"

"Yes."

"Okay. And once we were married, did we get counselling?"

"Yes, we did."

"And did that help?"

"No, it didn't."

"In fact, didn't it make our situation worse?"

"Yes, it did."

"Did you agree at the time that the counsellor was not doing what we needed? That she was not helping us find solutions for our problems?"

"That's right."

"And when I stopped going, did you continue to see the counsellor?"

"Yes, I did."

"And when you stopped seeing the counsellor, did you tell me that it had degenerated into a complaint session?"

"Yes, it did."

"After that effort at counselling, did I ask you to help us find another counsellor for us to see?"

"Yes."

"Did you find one for us?"

"No."

"Did you find a counsellor for the kids?"

"Yes, I did."

"And during our marriage, did I repeatedly ask you for your help in finding a counsellor to help us?"

"Yes."

"And was your answer always that you couldn't find a counsellor in Springfield who would accept your benefit plan?"

"Yes, it was."

"Did you ever try to find a counsellor outside Springfield?"

"No."

"And, have I ever struck you or the kids?"

"No, not really."

"Would you agree that, throughout our marriage, I've consistently asked you to help me find help for us, that I've repeatedly asked for help in dealing with my anger issues, and you've consistently refused to help me get access to medical treatment since that one effort at counselling?"

"Yes."

"Okay. That's it. I think I've made my point."

The judge then asked whether we had any final statements to make.

"Your Honor, I want him out of the house. He yells at me in front of the kids, and he yells and swears when he gets angry."

"Your Honor, Maria and I talked about my anger issues, and my need for help, before we ever got married. We agreed that we would all need counselling help for us to become a family, and that I needed help learning to deal with anger.

"After one failed attempt at counselling, Maria refused to help me find any other counselling options. I even asked her to show me what the benefit plan was so I could look for a counsellor, and she wouldn't do that.

"Now, here we are today. We both made this marriage, and we have both made mistakes. I don't think it's right or fair that I've been tossed out of my home, and that I'm being asked to pay the full freight for something that we've done together. I'm asking you to please deny this order of protection, let me go home, and please direct us to get counselling so we can work out our marriage."

There was a brief silence. For a moment, I thought I had made an impression.

"Mr. Hall, I think you're simply blaming the victim."

"Your Honor, that is not at all..."

He didn't even look at me. He just raised his hand like a king demanding silence.

"You've had your turn to speak.

"I'm granting the Plenary Order of Protection. I think you do represent a threat to Ms. Sanchez's safety, and there is this matter of having already violated the order of protection once. The Order of Protection is in effect for one year from today."

That was it. Maria was granted a Plenary Order of Protection. The judge claimed I was blaming the victim.

That's a common refrain – Maria is right and I'm wrong. Why is no one listening to how much it hurt to have my wife exclude me from everything? To have her tell me weeks or months after that one of the kids said something good about me to her? What point is there if no one is willing to hear the truth?

I wandered around town all afternoon in a daze.

In the evening, I went to the Christian Youth Center (the place where Pastor Cook's church meets on Sundays) and dropped off all my stuff to George, the fellow who runs the center. I told him it was a delivery for Pastor Cook.

I walked away from the building, and went straight to the bridge over the Illinois River. It's a one hundred foot drop into a fast running river. Drowning won't take long in December's cold.

All the way to the bridge, and while walking up to the highest point, I was talking to myself. Some of it out loud, some of it not. I kept wondering why it was that I kept getting shafted. I was definitely feeling sorry for myself.

But from the depths of that self-pity came a spark of anger. Why should I let all the people who have ever crapped on my win? If I kill myself, I thought, then they all get to be right.

Now, I'm the first guy in the world to admit that anger is a blunt instrument, and a poor tool. It has been at the root of most problems in my adult life. But if anger is all you have to hold onto, here is my advice: Hang on tight, and plan to pay the price later.

Anger is our emotional signal that something is wrong. There was definitely something wrong that night.

The night before, I had to face the fact that I couldn't keep going to counselling without a ride or money to pay for it. Today, I was told that the order of protection saying refrain doesn't matter, that I was blaming the victim, and that I would not be allowed to go home. Oh yes, there were a few things that felt wrong.

It's what you do with your anger that either makes the problem worse, or moves you toward a solution. I had no idea what my solution would be, but I decided suicide wasn't it. I was not going to go away and die just because people didn't want me around.

I went back to the Youth Center and asked George to speak with me outside. I told him I really left my stuff at the center because I had planned to commit suicide. I didn't share the details, and he didn't ask. What is truly important is that I told him I just don't have it in me to quit this way.

We talked for a little while, and although I didn't have a clear plan of action, I at least knew I was going to PADS that night instead of back to the bridge.

That evening at PADS, I'm arrested for "acting weird" and confined for psychiatric observation for 72 hours. I'm sent to Silver Cross Hospital.

Day 39 – Wednesday, 19 Dec

"Good morning, Donald. How are you today?"

Dr. Cosmé Lozano is about five foot seven, a little stout, with black wavy hair and well tanned skin. He's wearing the usual white doctor's coat, carrying a file folder, and seems fairly relaxed. That's about to change.

My voice is quiet, matter of fact, and I'm looking Dr. Lozano straight in the eye. "Conrad, actually."

"I beg your pardon?"

I explain quietly, in a voice that says I'm distinctly unhappy to be having this conversation. "My name is Conrad. I use my middle name."

Some tension creeps into Cosmé's voice now. "Okay. Conrad. I take it you're not particularly happy."

"Yes, and you have an amazing grasp of the obvious. Why on earth would you expect me to be happy?"

"That's what I'm here to find out. You know I'm here to help."

I share my perspective on that statement with a voice lacquered in scorn. "No, actually, you aren't."

"I'm not what?"

Now the anger starts coming out. "You're not here to help. You're here to dot the i's and cross the t's. You're here to fill in forms and justify your existence. The one thing you are most definitely not here to do is help."

"What makes you say that?"

"How about because you walk through the door with a cheery smile on your face, calling me by a name I don't use, and you start with an incredibly stupid, unthinking question. 'How am I doing?' I've been imprisoned for no good reason! How do you think I'm doing?"

Now, when you think about it, this probably isn't the harshest sort of thing a doctor in a psychiatric wing has had said to him, right? But Cosmé was getting a little cheesed off.

"We're really just here to help."

That just pissed me off. My voice got louder and harder. "No, you aren't. Everybody has been saying that to me since I was tackled by three cops last night."

I sneered and attacked him with a whiny voice, 'We're just trying to help.'

"The nurse and doctor at the hospital kept saying it last night. They said it every time I caught them in a lie. 'We're just trying to help.'

"Everybody's just trying to help. So you arrest me, you confine me against my will, you tell me if I'm not a good little boy, you'll pump me full of drugs and maybe strap electrodes to my head. But you're just trying to help.

"Face it, Doctor, you don't know what help is. All you know is filling forms and pushing pills."

That little tirade, while momentarily gratifying and entirely accurate, was not what Cosmé wanted to hear. He let his frustration show.

"Listen, if you don't want my help, just say so. I can have you out of here tomorrow morning."

"I don't think so."

"Certainly. I can have the paperwork done today, and you'll be out of here by tomorrow morning."

I shook my head in disagreement. My voice was clear and back to being an indoor voice. "No, you can't. In fact, that would be a very bad idea."

His eyebrows went up and his eyes widened at that. "Why is that?"

"Because I was sent here on a seventy-two hour commitment. If you let me go early, that means I'm right and everyone else involved is wrong. That means I get to sue their asses into the next century.

"No, I don't think you're going to let me go. I don't belong here; that's right. I should never have been tackled by the police, arrested or confined, but I was. And now you're stuck holding the bag.

"You can't let me go without causing a whole lot of problems."

Cosmé was in an interesting spot. Yes, everyone in Springfield had made a mistake. He could see they had committed someone for observation without good reason, but he couldn't just let me go. He decided to stop arguing and just go with the truth.

"You know what? You're right. I can't let you go

"So since we're here together, and you don't think I can help, what are we going to do?"

I looked him up and down, and thought for a minute before answering. When I did, my intention was to discover whether Dr. Lozano just might be helpful.

"Hmmm... A much better approach," I said slowly.

"The truth is: I don't know whether you can help me or not. I know for certain that no one from last night can be of help because they did nothing to be helpful. They didn't make any effort to listen. Worse. They assumed everything I said was a lie to avoid being committed."

In a softer voice, I said "Ironic that. They are so

steeped in telling lies, and claiming they're helping, they can't imagine anyone telling the truth."

I snapped back from my reflective attitude, and addressed Cosmé again.

"I don't know whether you have the ability to be of help to me or not, but I'm willing to find out."

That was the start of a ninety minute conversation; far longer than Cosmé had intended being with me. In the end, we were willing to "give it a try" as it were.

He understood that I needed him to hear what I was saying instead of hearing what he expected to hear. I understood he needed me to be open about myself, and continue being honest and straightforward with him.

We would end up talking together a lot over the next few days.

Day 41 – Friday, 21 Dec

Today is the end of the seventy-two hour commitment. Technically, they have to let me go tomorrow, but that's Saturday. The people who do the release paperwork don't work weekends, so they have to get it done this afternoon.

The person responsible for getting the paperwork done is a social worker named Lynette. She's a nice lady. I haven't participated in any of the therapeutic activities that go on each day, but I've talked with Lynette and Dr. Lozano.

Lynette came to me in the morning to talk about being released, but she had another option in mind. She had asked me to meet her in the dining room, and was waiting for me when I arrived.

Lynette is a small lady; about five foot one, with a cheerleader's physique. She was always cheerful when she spoke, and listened well. Her main function is helping people connect with resources and family when they leave Silver Cross Hospital. Since I had neither, and was there unwillingly, mine was a problematic situation. "Hi, Conrad. Are you looking forward to leaving today?"

I, on the other hand, was not generally cheerful when I spoke. "Hmmm... Let me think for a second... I was sent here against my will, and imprisoned without cause. An assessment with which Cosmé agrees, and I've been kept here so the people who screwed up and sent me here incorrectly can't be sued.

"Yes, I think you could say I'm looking forward to leaving."

I sat down across a table from Lynette while I spoke. She had a file folder with her that held notes about me.

"Conrad, I know you're not happy about being here. You've made that clear, and I understand why you're angry. I'd be angry, too, if my freedom were suddenly taken away."

In other circumstances, I probably would not have listened to what seems like drivel. But Lynette was mostly straightforward with me, and always willing to come clean if I called her on something.

"If you want to leave, we'll get your paperwork done and you can go today. But I'd like you to think about another option. Can I tell you what I'm thinking about?"

My eyebrows came up at the suggestion of another option. I knew in my gut that the only thing she could be considering was me staying longer. That was not something I was particularly open to, but she was attractive and nice.

"No, I'm not particularly interested, but okay, go

ahead and tell me. I'll listen."

"Good.

"What I'm thinking is that Christmas is just a few days away, and you've said you don't much like Christmas. There's also the fact that you don't really have anywhere to go. Now, I know this isn't the best place in the world, but there's a fairly nice Christmas dinner, and I'd feel a lot better knowing you're here.

"Would you consider staying until after Christmas?"

I said I'd listen, and I did. Now I was thinking about what she had said. It was December, and leaving would only put me back at PADS. Most of the places where I was spending time each day would be closed.

"Okay. I get what you're saying.

"I stay here, and I'm warm, have a roof over my head, and three meals a day. I get it.

"But this place is set up to treat people like kids. We have to do things to your timetable, and when I don't cooperate I get warned that a bad note is going to be made in my chart." I was on a bit of a roll already, and let out some of my frustration for a system that claims to help, but is only idiotic.

"And what's worse is you do things that are incredibly stupid and dangerous. I'll even give you an example." I can't imagine Lynette was happy about what I was saying, but I give her full credit for genuinely listening.

"You won't let anyone have a pen. Why I don't know. Instead, you want everyone to use a pencil. Now, what is incredibly stupid is that you use the short, golf-style pencil. Have you ever really thought about that?" Lynette shook her head, and I continued.

"Here are a bunch of emotionally distressed people. People who are very unhappy, and who might be thinking about hurting themselves or someone else. And here is the medical establishment, in its infinite wisdom, equipping those people with an ideal concealed weapon." Lynette was surprised by this idea.

"You've never thought of that, have you?" I picked up one of the pencils that happened to be on the table. I leaned forward and held it in the palm of my hand.

"Here you have a nice, pointy object. And when I close my hand, it disappears, doesn't it? So down the hall I come, pencil hidden in my hand, and before you know it, I put my thumb over the end to hold it firmly, and can tear out your throat in seconds.

"If I were you, I think I'd prefer a pen. At least that can't be hidden so easily. And if you want to stick with pencils, I'd be using those big, thick, red pencils they give out in grade two.

"That's just one example, and you want me to stay here." I put the pencil back on the table.

"Even with being warm, sheltered from the elements and meals, why should I? You folks think you're here to help, but you're not. You're just going through the motions and don't even realise it."

"Wow. I haven't thought about the pencils that way before. You're right. They could be quite dangerous. I'll mention it, too, but I'd appreciate it if you told this to Dr. Lozano when you see him next. It's something worth thinking about." She paused and was looking at the pencil.

"Conrad, you're right. I don't have a reason beyond my concern for you over the holidays. I'd like you to seriously consider staying until after Christmas."

"I have thought about it. I've been thinking about it since you mentioned it, and I have an answer.

"I'll stay... but I have conditions. You meet them, I'll stay."

Every other patient on that floor was there because they wanted to be there. They had signed themselves in, and had asked for help. They followed direction, and participated in the group activities. Even though the doors are locked and you can't leave, a place feels less like a prison when you can sign yourself out. A patient offering to negotiate was new for everyone.

"Obviously I can't promise anything, but I'll do my best."

"That's fine. I understand, but this is where I'm at: You folks meet my conditions, I stay. You don't, I'm gone. So here it is…"

I started talking, Lynette started making notes, and my guess is that we were both thinking very quickly.

"Being here is of no use to me at all if I can't keep working my book. That book is my next step in healing. It's my way of closing old wounds, sorting out what I'm responsible for, and what I can do something about. So if I'm going to stay, I want access to my book. I want to be able to work.

"Now, what I'd really like is for you to let me use my laptop, but I doubt that's going to happen. I want you to ask, but I don't expect that to work.

"What I do need are my notes. There's a binder full of notes in my backpack that I can work with. The outline for the book is there, and there are lots of notes on the Kickstarter that I can work on.

"And I want a pen. Stop treating me like a child. Let me use the pens and highlighters that are in my backpack. I have those little post-it notes for bookmarking pages, let me use those. And I want my bible. I don't claim to agree with God on everything that's in there, but there's lots of wisdom in its pages. And I take comfort from reading it.

"That's what I want. You get me access to my notes, let me work on my book, and I'll stay, otherwise I'm just wasting time."

I sat back in my chair and waited for an answer. Lynette thought for a bit, then gave the beginning of an answer.

"This is an unusual request. You're right about the laptop. They're not likely to agree to that.

"I agree with what you're saying. It makes sense for you to be working on something while you're here, but I can't just say yes to this. Even Dr. Lozano can't just say yes. The head nurse has to approve something like this. So here's what I'll do…

"I think this is a good idea. I'll talk to Dr. Lozano, and we'll talk to the head nurse. I can't make any promises, but we'll have an answer for you in a couple of hours."

Lynette was back with an answer just after lunch.

I was the first psychiatric patient in the history of Silver Cross to be given access to personal belongings during their stay. I didn't get my laptop, but they let me have my notes, pens, highlighters and post-it notes.

Their return conditions were that I work on my notes in front of the nurse's station. They didn't want me taking all that stuff off to my room where other patients might get access to a pen. I was also given access to my journal. And Lynette asked me to make an effort at attending some of the group sessions.

This makes me happier than I've been in weeks. it feels good to have someone work with me instead of against me.

This is from a journal entry on Christmas Eve:

Over the last few days, I've put a lot of effort into looking at what happened during our marriage. My effort has been focussed on ACCURATELY writing down what happened, taking responsibility for what I have done AND what I could have done differently, and being clear about what Maria did WITHOUT assigning blame to her.

I think we will be divorced. Maria has her heart and mind set on this, and I am now willing to move in that direction. My intention is to obtain legal help so I'm correctly represented, and let Maria have the divorce.

I made the effort to attend some of the group sessions. It was a more positive experience than I had imagined, and I got to know a little more about the other people on the floor.

Day 45 – Tuesday, 25 Dec

This is the first time I write in my journal that I'm prepared to move on without Maria.

I think I can make something of my life. I haven't felt like this in more than a year, and certainly not since Maria filed for divorce. There are things I'm still afraid of – being alone, an uncertain future, the challenge of the book – but I think I can make it. My faith in God is re-growing, and I realise part of my mistake was ignoring the support and comfort faith brings to your life.

It's surprising to be happy on Christmas. I have some real bad memories of it from childhood, and as an adult I've mostly been alone and lonely during the holidays. Today I'm thinking of the real love and compassion I've seen in Maria during the holidays. I remember taking pictures of each of the kids when we wrapped them up in Christmas lights, and how much we enjoyed each other. I wish we could all go back to that happy time and start over from there.

I should have kissed the kids more often and made more effort to hug them. I have an intense fear of rejection and I know it. Yet I allowed it to control me. If I ever get a second chance (hopefully with Maria and the kids) I'm better prepared to do it differently; to love them better.

Day 46 – Wednesday, 26 Dec

I'm released from Silver Cross Hospital and return to Springfield, IL. It's a relief to have my freedom. As productive as the days at Silver Cross were – and they were – I was still confined. It's hard to believe that a few weeks ago (before jail and psychiatric confinement) I never really thought to thank God for being free. It's so true that losing a thing sometimes makes you appreciate it more when you get it back.

Going back into PADS is a little frightening. Having experience the reaction of volunteers and guests after being in jail – it didn't matter that I was jailed for telling Maria I love her – I'm afraid for how they'll react to me now.

Cosmé's advice is still in my ears: Keep focussed on your own progress and doing what's necessary to be happy each day. It makes me determined to write Getting Happy…when you wish you were dead. I'm convinced sharing my experience can help other people have an easier time of it.

Still, I wish I could go back to the safety and security of Silver Cross – even though it means having less freedom. I wish I could hold Maria and share my passion, fears and ambition with her.

Day 49 – Saturday, 29 Dec

I get my first prescription for Ritalin filled. It cost $4. There's only a 15 day supply – enough to get me through until I see Cosmé at his office.

I start putting together details for a Kickstarter.com campaign. This is how I originally planned to get Getting Happy...when you wish you were dead published.

On the one hand, I feel defeated because I'm back on Ritalin. I am fortunate that most of the ADD symptoms can be controlled with a careful combination of diet, exercise and rest. This came apart during our marriage, and I cannot re-establish my routine while in PADS. So the Ritalin is necessary, though unwelcome.

On the other hand, I have a vision and the plan for achieving it. I want to find teenagers who are as I once was, and keep them from travelling the dark paths I have walked. Talking with Cosmé, I've realised that Getting Happy...when you wish you were dead can help a lot of people. Perhaps God gave me my history – especially these days of divorce, disgrace, anger and anguish – to make me into someone who can honestly help others.

People have always sort of laughed at my motto of Cranium Ex Rectum. But in a world where no one expects to be held accountable, maybe it's time for someone to say "Pull your head out of your arse" and take responsibility for yourself. That's what Getting Happy is all about – shedding the guilt other people want to pile on me while taking full responsibility for what I have done. It's making me a better, happier man.

I pray that one day I'll be able to share this with someone who becomes my wife.

Day 53 – Wednesday, 2 Jan

My first appointment with Matthew Parks at Batterdrum Mental Health. He does the intake paperwork to get me started with counselling.

Today I gave up hope of reconciling with Maria. It's what I want, but I'm convinced it won't happen. I write in my journal "I've pretty much given up even thinking of reconciliation with Maria. She wants help – she has asked so often. But if God hasn't softened her heart by now, I don't know that He will. I'll try talking to Maria's lawyer, but I confess to having little hope."

Day 55 – Friday, 4 Jan – Confused, Suicidal, Despair

My emotions are out of control. I write in my journal "In my heart and mind, there is still a strong hope that Maria and I will find a life together." I'm confused and hurt. I want to let go and move on. At the same time, I feel crushed and weakened from being rejected.

Day 59 – Tuesday, 8 Jan – Stressed, Doubtful, Wanting to Quit

The first hearing for the divorce. It is simply continued to 15 Jan because I'm having a first meeting with a lawyer Friday. That's unlikely to go far because I have no money to pay a lawyer, but at least I can ask for help.

A hearing on the violation of order of protection. It is continued until February. We're waiting to see if Karen from the Diversion Program will approve what I'm doing at Batterdrum Mental Health.

Having both issues in one day is hard. The court process is incredibly intimidating because it's completely unfamiliar.

Karen runs a Diversion Program in some kind of partnership with the courts. The idea is that you go to some lessons about why it's wrong to fight with your spouse instead of going to jail. Sounds okay so far, right? I mean, I had already been trying to work on my anger issues so I'm cool with anything that helps me do that.

The catch is that the Diversion Program has a cost attached to it: $1,500.00. And you have to pay that fee. If you can't afford it, you're not eligible and you go to jail.

Well, Maria has all the funds and all my assets. I'm clearly not eligible.

I was already seeing Matthew Parks at Batterdrum Mental Health, and they offer quite a few group counseling sessions. So Matthew helped me find out what is covered in the Diversion Program, and I signed up for several of the group counseling sessions.

Then we put together a proposal for Karen showing how the counseling at Batterdrum Mental Health achieves the same results as the Diversion Program. If Karen accepts Batterdrum Mental Health as a valid alternative, then I can get help and avoid jail.

The big difference between the two is that services at Batterdrum Mental Health are free. If Karen says the counseling there is a valid alternative, then her business loses a $1,500 fee. It also sets a precedent that might allow other people to dodge that fee.

This is why covering everything in one day is hard, tiring and intimidating. It's a little hard to believe Karen is going to approve a counseling option that loses money for her business.

Day 60 – Wednesday, 9 Jan

"You know, I've been thinking about the e-mail you sent me and your concern about taking on too much. I think you might be right." I had sent Matthew an e-mail saying I was eager to learn, and was just a little concerned about being in seven group sessions at once. I had asked to talk more about it during this appointment.

"Right about what? That I'm concerned?" I joked.

Without waiting for Matthew to reply, "In any case, I've put a lot of time and thought into it. Yes, it's going to be a lot of work. I think most of my trepidation is around the idea of having to put in the effort, and then there's the thought of having to meet and deal with all those new people.

"But I think it's the right thing to do. If there's any opportunity to have that court program approve what I'm doing over their own diversion program, then what I'm doing had better be complete. And I'm not one to things by half measure.

I was smiling and clearly enthusiastic about my decision. "So I'm good with tackling the whole deal. It's going to be a lot of work, but it's going to be worth it."

"Are you sure about that? I really think you'd be better off cutting back, and just being in two or three groups to start."

"Okay. I get it," I said calmly; prepared to explain my position again. "But you're leading two of the groups, and I'll still be seeing you privately like this. As long as you and I keep seeing each other regularly, I should be able to handle anything that's coming up during group sessions."

Matthew paused, and looked a little like he was chewing a sour candy. "Well, I was hoping you'd be happy about the idea of cutting back on the group sessions."

"Why?"

"We had a staff meeting earlier today, and we talked about your concerns and how much you're taking on. Some of the other counselors were also concerned about you getting the benefit of so many resources at once, and we agreed that you should cut back on the number of groups you're attending."

I was still slouching in my seat, but I was no longer relaxed and enthusiastic. "Wait a second... All of you talked about what I should and should not be doing, then made a decision about me without even talking to me about it? And you were hoping I'd be happy about that?"

"It's not just the counselors. Some of the other group participants expressed concern about you being in the groups. One person is intimidated by you, and one of the other participants thinks you're just in the group to get material for your book."

Feeling sarcastic and disgusted, "Right. Only if I were there to get material for a book, I would never have mentioned the book in the first place."

"I mentioned that to him."

"And isn't the point of group sessions to work at dealing with things that bother you? What's the point of being there if you, the counselors, are going to remove all the obstacles?" Matthew was, I think, waiting for the storm to blow over. He didn't make any effort to answer.

"So because it's easier for you, and because you think I'm getting some kind of unfair advantage by being willing to do the extra work, you've all decided I have to cut back on the number of group sessions. You make this decision without talking to me, you expect me to be happy about it, and it sure seems like I don't have any choice in the matter. So how am I supposed to trust any of you?"

"I understand you being upset. I thought since you told me you were concerned about how much you were taking on, it would be good to help you make the decision. So we've decided which three groups you can attend."

I was utterly overwhelmed by the callousness at this point. My voice was flat as I replied, "Wow. Not only have you decided that I have to cut back, you're also telling me which groups to attend. I'm overwhelmed by the love and support you're communicating." (Sarcasm comes easily when you're thoroughly miffed.)

Rather than be subjected to such inconsistency, I choose to remove myself from all group therapy. Betrayal in this environment is not easy to accept.

I wonder if there's ever anybody I can trust. This really motivates me to keep looking at what is truly my responsibility when it comes to Maria and me. I keep wondering whether I'll ever get it right.

In the middle of talking to Matthew, and thinking all of this, I'm hit with a flashback. If you've never had one, they're intense memories. A flashback usually lasts just a few seconds, but it plays out an entire memory that may have taken minutes to experience.

~

We were walking across the front lawn, headed who knows where, and Joe was nattering at me. As an older brother, he was always crowing about being in charge. And all younger siblings know, that's irritating every time it happens.

This time, I'd had enough. Joe shoved me from behind, and I got mad. When I spun around to yell at him, I noticed two things. It struck me that we were almost the same size. He was three years older, but I was almost as big as him. And the other thing – he had stepped back. My big brother was afraid.

There was no way I was going to lose again. Joe had the advantage, sure. He was 11 and three years older than me; my big brother. But I was almost the same size as him, and had my fill of being pushed around whenever our parents were there to back him up. This time it was just us on the front lawn, with nobody to back either of us.

We wrestled, we punched, and we fought with words.

"You're no good. You know I'm going to win," he grunted as we wrestled. The grass dug into our skin right through our shirts as we fought. Our Dad always wanted the grass cut golf course short so that made it dry and brittle. It never got watered as much as a golf course.

"I've had enough of your shit," as I punched him in the stomach. The rage was boiling out of me. Hitting his stomach felt like punching bread dough. I thought my hand would go all the way through, and part of me wanted it to happen. The wind came whooshing out of him. Then I rolled us over and landed on top, so I scrambled to sit on his chest. I punched him in the face again and again.

"You might be older, and they might not want me around," I growled as I sat firmly on his chest, "but you're gonna stop bossing me," my fist was an exclamation mark on his head, "or I'm gonna beat you silly." It hadn't hurt much when I punched him in the face, but this time I hit him in the side of the head. The jolt went all the way up to my shoulder. Instead of rocking to the side, his whole head went sideways like he was touching his ear to his shoulder. A sense of victory and power flooded through me.

Suddenly the fight stopped. I had won. Or maybe it's more right to say I realized I had won, and there was no more need to hit. How very different life might have been had I simply taken the victory and stood up then, but I didn't.

It felt good sitting on my brother's chest. He was trying to get me off and couldn't. It was my first victory, and I was enjoying the sensation of feeling bigger and stronger. I didn't have to hit him anymore; he was crushed and we both knew it. I could see it in his face. I felt like the king of the world. I knew I wouldn't have to take any more of his crap.

Then something crashed into me and the world went black.

When I woke up, I saw I was clear across on the other side of the flower bed; maybe fifteen feet from where we'd been fighting. My father was picking Joe up, dusting him off and helping him stand.

It didn't surprise me that our dad had intervened. Our parents always made it clear I was second rate; someone to be tolerated or ordered about. It didn't even surprise me that my father – a 250 lb man – had knocked me flying. It wasn't the first time. But it was the first time I had won a fight. It was the first time he'd had to clobber me to save Joe.

I rolled up onto my left side and watched our dad brush off Joe's back and pants. As I started to get up, I knew it was all over. My world – my victory – was finished. I would never be allowed to win, to succeed. It was unfair. I knew that. And I felt a hole open inside me.

"You want a fight?" he asked as he put his arm around Joe's shoulders. "Now come fight us," he said in a fit of anger and wounded pride. He had just seen his son beaten, and not by a neighborhood bully or some worthy opponent. No, his son had been beaten by me; the dirty third. The kid they had to keep in the family because he was born there. The one who was never supposed to be good for anything except taking up space.

There stood my big brother with a happy, surprised, what just happened? look on his face. With our father's arm around Joe's shoulders, that bewilderment shifted into haughtiness. He crossed his arms. The look on his face said I can beat you now.

"Right, and I'm supposed to come fight the two of you. Like that's fair," I said in shock and dismay. The hole opening inside me was rimmed with betrayal. It was one thing to stop a fight, but this felt like being disowned. That's what made the hole: I had just lost my family.

In a last ditch effort to save something of my self, an idea came to me from all the movies and TV shows I'd seen. "Sometimes a brave man knows when to walk away from a fight," I said, trying to hurt my father at the same time that I hid my own pain and tears.

Then I turned and started walking up the sidewalk. I figured I'd walk away to let things cool off. I didn't know how long it would take before I'd be able to go home. And I had no idea whether there would be a punishment waiting for me when I got there.

We lived across the street from a big railroad yard. It was good because it taught me to sleep through anything, and it was always an interesting place to play and explore.

Now it looked different. The main part of the yard was filled with freight trains. They always moved slowly. I didn't care about them. But between our house and the main yard was a small gully. Two sets of tracks ran through it for the Amtrak trains.

They moved fast.

After I walked a little way up the block, I crossed the street. There was just a field between us and the railroad yard. No fences.

I walked across the field thinking. Joe would be unbearable now. Clearly I was not part of the family. Nobody wanted me.

I walked down into the gully and sat on the tracks. I thought about how fast the trains moved, and wished for one to come. I picked up stones just to throw them. I laid my ear on the rails to listen for a train.

I waited.

I wished for a train.

~

I came back to the room with barely a twitch. I took a deep breath, sat up a little, and focused on Matthew. How long was I gone? Had Matthew said anything, or asked me something? I don't know. He was simply sitting in his chair looking at me.

"Okay. I think I've heard everything you've said. But here's the thing: You and the other counsellors made the decision based on what serves you best, not me. So, from my perspective, you can't be trusted.

"My answer is that I'm out of all the groups.

There's no benefit in trying to work with people who can't be trusted."

At this point, Matthew got a little angry. He was clearly upset by what I had said.

"It sounds like you're saying you don't want to be here anymore."

"I don't know. You've certainly taken the wind out of my sails."

"Okay. Let me ask you this: Do you feel you can trust me enough as a counsellor for me to be of benefit to you?"

"I don't know, Matthew. I have to think about it."

"Well, in that case, I'll just close your file."

This struck a chord of fear for me. That I was attending counselling sessions had already been mentioned in court. Matthew knew that. What would it mean if I stopped attending? And since Matthew was clearly angry with me, I had little hope that he would be kind or helpful in how he communicated with the court.

"I don't know. I didn't say 'close my file.' I just need time to think about it."

I left the office feeling worried and pressured. I didn't want to work with Matthew anymore, but I had the court process to think about. Working with him could also provide good material for *Getting*

Happy... when you wish you were dead. At the very least, he could be an example of the sort of counsellor to avoid.

Day 66 – Tuesday, 15 Jan – Angry, Frustrated, Impotent

There's another hearing for the divorce today.

The judge refuses to give me more time to find a lawyer. Instead, he tells me to work out a settlement with Maria's lawyer.

When I raise the point that Maria's lawyer is hardly likely to have any care or concern for my best interests, he agrees.

"You're right. She isn't paid to look out for your interests; she paid to look after her client. So go talk to her, and see what you can work out."

He then adjourned the proceedings until January 22.

When I spoke with Joan Harrop, Maria's lawyer, outside the courtroom, she was confrontational and belligerent. She said she's all on Maria's side and what I want doesn't matter.

Maria and I really did have our problems. I'd like to sit down and work them out, but that was one of our problems – we just didn't communicate very well. It feels like everyone is lined up against me. That's what gets me feeling angry and frustrated. And my lack of knowledge about how the courts work gets me feeling impotent.

There has to be a better way to get through this. What I feel is my choice, so how do I choose to feel differently? Can I really be happy even when everything feels like it's going against me?

I also had a meeting with Matthew Parks today. I still won't be attending group sessions. I'm certain I can get value from them, but I'm equally certain my feelings toward the staff would result in my being adversarial. That isn't fair to them, me or the other participants.

Matthew was smart enough to ask again whether I trust him enough for him to be effective as a therapist. I remembered Cosmé's advice about being careful with what I say to other mental health professionals. I'm willing to give him a second chance because I need/want his help with the book.

Day 67 – Wednesday, 16 Jan – Fearful, Grateful and a little Hopeful

I volunteer at We Care for the first time. This is the local food bank in Batterdrum County. I went because I had forgotten something at PADS and knew it would be brought to We Care. One of the volunteers told me all the lost and found items get taken to We Care. It hadn't arrived by the time I got there, so I volunteered to lend a hand if I could be useful.

That turned into 2 ½ hours of helping. It felt good to be useful.

I attend the Bible Study at Living Water church. Pastor Stan Pear is not there, and Ben Fields runs the study. Ben is the one who originally invited me to attend, and I was a little worried because Maria also attends that study. But Ben said she hadn't been coming and there should be no conflict.

Maria wasn't there so everything was fine. It wasn't going to stay that way.

Day 71 – Sunday, 20 Jan – Peaceful, Thoughtful

Dan and Karen Peterson were volunteers at one of the PADS locations. I didn't know it when we first started talking, but their son had committed suicide. So they had a particular interest on my view of things, and what I was doing with the book.

They must have liked what I was saying well enough because I was invited to attend the memorial for their son – Gary Stump. It felt strange to be in so much pain myself, and still be giving solace to people who are essentially strangers.

I had a lot of conversations with PADS volunteers about suicide. I remember one conversation in particular where a male volunteer told me he didn't understand how people could think about suicide.

"If I were getting that kind of discouragement and abuse, I would have just gone somewhere else."

"Right. So at seven, eight, nine years of age, where do you go? How do you even get past believing your parents, the people filling your head with this stuff your whole life, are right? How do you tell a child to walk away from his parents? And where is he supposed to go, anyway?"

I also told him about asking to go live with Aunt Geri.

The summer after I had called home to share my success with Mom, I didn't get shipped off to Aunt Bessie's or the Sager's. My parents started sending me to live Grandma Charters for half the summer, and Aunt Geri the other half. It was during the second summer at Aunt Geri's, when I was eight, that I asked to live with her.

"Aunt Geri, can I come live with you?"

"Why would you want that, Conrad?" Aunt Geri always used people's names. She didn't use honey, dear or other pet names for people. She paid attention to people, and used their names.

"I like it here. And besides, Mom and Dad don't want me around, so they won't care if I'm gone."

Little did I know that this was not quite true.

"You'll have to ask your mother. If she says yes, then it's okay with me."

Grandma lived about two hours away from us, and Aunt Geri was almost six hours away. Mom would drive me to Grandma's then Aunt Geri would pick me up from Grandma's. Mom came out to Aunt Geri's at the end of the summer to bring me home for school. I always thought I was a bit strange for not having developed the same childhood friendships that other people have, but I guess it's kind of hard when you're away so much.

You might be surprised at how blunt a child can be. Then again, kids do say the darndest things. Oddly, in addition to making me a practiced liar, living with parents who casually bent the truth also gave me a lack of consideration for how other people felt. When my mother arrived at the end of the summer, I was a little afraid to ask but I eventually approached the subject directly.

"Aunt Geri, did you ask her?"

"Did I ask her what?" We were in the kitchen, and my mother was in the dining room. She was easily visible through the door, but far enough away to not hear a quiet conversation.

"Did you ask Mom if I can come live with you?"

"No. it's not for me to ask."

I just looked at her, and silently wished for a different answer.

"Conrad, if you want to live here, you have to ask your mother. I'm happy to have you live here, and I'll talk to her after you ask, but it's up to you to go ask her first."

Aunt Geri and Grandma Charters were both no-nonsense people who spoke directly. They also had a lot of love and patience to share. There were lots of occasions when both of them had hard words for me, but there wasn't a single time when I didn't feel loved by them.

I worked up the courage to ask my mother about living at Aunt Geri's.

"Mom, can I come live with Aunt Geri?"

"Why would you want to do that?"

"Well, she doesn't have any kids, and I like being here, so that's good. And besides, you and Dad obviously don't want me around, and Aunt Geri says she'd be happy to have me live here."

In the end, the answer was no. The reason given was that Uncle Harold (Aunt Geri's husband) said no. What no one ever knew was that I had asked Uncle Harold first. He had said yes, but that it was really up to Aunt Geri.

The PADS volunteer didn't have any more answers after I finished the story. He still didn't understand how anyone could think about suicide, and that's a good thing. If every person felt the same way, it would mean that no one would ever think about suicide.

Day 75 – Thursday, 24 Jan – Shocked and Amused

Matthew Parks is at PADS tonight. Naturally our conversation touches on mental illness and I make the point that I have no organic mental illness. He then informs me that "being in his community" automatically entitles me to a diagnosis of PTSD. An interesting point is that Matthew has done absolutely nothing to evaluate me for signs and symptoms of PTSD. He bases the diagnosis solely on my having had a traumatic childhood and life.

This is surprising, and a little amusing. It fits with what Dr. Lozano has warned me about, and with what I've read from Dr. William Glasser and Dr. Terry Lynch. They've both written books about fulfilling personal needs and changing your behaviors.

We all tend to reach conclusions that support our view of the world. It takes consistent effort to check what you're thinking against what is true.

It makes me think of a conversation I once had with a group of university students. I don't have a degree, but I've spent a lot of time at universities talking with students, participating in their radio programs, and doing continuing education courses.

One time, I was having a conversation with about half a dozen students about common misconceptions. Now, you'd think that would be a dead giveaway, but not quite.

I told them that people often argue about which will hit the ground first: a ten pound weight, or a one pound weight. Every student immediately said the ten pound weigh would hit first.

They argued strenuously when I corrected them and said the weights would strike the ground at the same time.

You're welcome to look it up if you're interested. There was a certain science-type guy who figured this out by dropping weights from a tower a few hundred years ago.

That led us to talking about truth, so naturally I asked them whether absolute truth exists. Just as naturally, and very quickly, they answered with there's no such thing as absolute truth. After I gave them a few examples like, water expands when it freezes - and is the only substance that does. Water cannot be compressed, gasses expand to fill the available volume, and little brothers are always a nuisance. Then I capped the conversation by saying "So you're telling me there's absolutely no such thing as absolute truth."

That finally broke through their scepticism.

Most of the problems I've had in life have come about because I wouldn't live with another person's illusions. My parents always complained that I wouldn't listen. I complained that I never knew when to believe them, and that the rules changed from day to day. Girlfriends have found me demanding when I insist that lying for any reason - even to arrange a surprise party - is wrong.

Like those university students, most people are living with things that aren't true. They're also quite likely to argue in favor of those false beliefs if challenged.

Day 79 – Monday, 28 Jan – Saddened AND Energized

Met with Matthew Parks today. He seems committed to the idea that I'm mentally ill rather than unhappy and under a lot of stress. I really have to start recording the sessions or making notes. I'm afraid of the power Matthew wields to have someone committed.

It was sad to feel pushed to be ill, but we did do some good talking today. Matthew likes the idea of me keeping a journal. I've done it off and on for years, and right now it's helping a lot to write things down.

Naturally we talk a lot about my past. Matthew and I agree that what has passed is precisely that – the past. You can't do anything about it. Yet he seems to phrase things as though I'm behaving like a victim of my past. That feels odd because I've never perceived myself as a victim. Yes, bad things have happened to me. I am the person I am today because of all my experiences, but I don't think I use that as an excuse or crutch.

When I say this to Matthew, he gets upset. He claims I'm not appreciating what he's doing for me. His phrasing takes me back to a similar situation with my father and brother.

There was a model jet fighter I was trying to put together. It was a large model with wings made to move forward and back for different flying configurations, and I was having a lot of trouble getting it to go together.

My father was sitting in the living room reading, and I was building the model on the coffee table just a couple of feet away.

My fairly frequent complaints of "This is just not going together," must have caught his attention.

"Then leave it alone. You're never going to get it together anyway."

That went straight through to my heart. I put everything down and walked out of the living room to go to my bedroom. Joe and I shared a bedroom, and he was sitting at his desk working on something.

"That model is just not going together." It had been the highlight of my Christmas presents, so Joe knew exactly what I was talking about.

He turned in his chair to see me, and asked "What's not working?"

"Oh, I can't get the wings to go on right."

"Maybe try reading through the instructions again."

"I don't know why I bother trying. I'll never amount to anything anyway."

Within seconds of saying that, I was slammed backward onto the bed. My father stood over me growling "Don't ever let me hear you talk like that again."

I spent the rest of the evening in our bedroom.

The next morning, I walked into the living room to find the model completed.

"Way cool! Who put this together?"

My father was in the kitchen eating breakfast. "Your brother and I put it together last night after you gave up. Be sure to say thank you."

I grabbed up the model and tried the wings. They moved just the way they were supposed to. I immediately went buzzing down the hallway to our bedroom.

"Thank you! This is way cool!"

My brother was a little surprised by my bursting into the room, but he also looked a little embarrassed. "You're welcome. I'm glad you like it."

I spent the next hours flying the plane around the living room. It dived, soared, buzzed the coffee table, and flew past the windows. The wings changing for every dive and climb, and spreading wide for level flight. Until finally, something clicked inside the model and the wings wouldn't move.

I tried everything I could think of to make the wings move again. When I couldn't get them to move, I quietly put the model back on the coffee table.

As I was leaving the living room, my father lowered his book and asked "Why aren't you playing with your model?"

I knew there was no point trying to hide anything. "I think I might have broke it. The wings won't move."

"That's typical. You just have to play with things until you break them. You don't appreciate anything your brother or I do for you."

I went to our bedroom and read until supper. I had learned to stay out of the way whenever anything bad happened. When Mom called all of us to supper, I noticed the model had landed in the garbage.

It makes me sad that my therapist is taking the same approach. He tells me I'm behaving like a victim, and when I give him current examples that show that's not true, he claims I don't appreciate what he's doing for me. It's a hard spot to be in.

The most important thing any of us can do is be honest with ourselves about who we are, what we've done, and what we are doing. I'm finally headed in that direction, but it's hard to know whether I'm on the right track.

Day 80 – Tuesday, 29 Jan – Exultant and Encouraged

Last week, after the Wednesday evening bible study, Ben Fields and I spent some time talking about the Getting Happy… book project. It caught his interest, and we arranged to meet this evening at the Pancake House.

"Hi, gentlemen. Can I get you something to drink?"

Ben gestured for me to go first. "May I have hot tea, please?"

"Okay. And for you?"

'Coffee, please."

The waitress bustled off to get our drinks.

"So tell me more about this project you're working on."

"I'm happy to," I answered as I pulled a small sheaf of papers from my laptop bag. "I also typed up an executive summary, and the plan as it is now."

I handed the papers over to Ben, and continued explaining.

"This is a piece of a larger project I was working on when things went south between Maria and me. The idea is to start with a single book, see how it's received, and then proceed with a series if the response is good.

"The series title is Getting Happy…, and the first book in the series is Getting Happy… when you wish you were dead. It's based on my life experience, and the fact that I'm still here. What I want to do is show people it is possible to survive. That there's hope, or a light at the end of the tunnel; even though you might not see it because there are some bends in the tunnel ahead of you."

"Okay. And what do you want from me?"

"Well, if you can help with the project, that's great, but mostly I'd like to have your feedback.

"You see, I've been working on this without anyone to talk to, so I could use an objective opinion. I'd like you to tell me whether it looks reasonable, it looks not so good, or maybe I'm in desperate need of medication."

We both laughed, and Ben agreed to share his opinion.

Our drinks arrived, and we ordered food. It was late in the evening, but we both asked for breakfast items. I had the pancake sandwich; two pancakes with a ham steak between them, top with two scrambled eggs. Ben went simpler with eggs, bacon, home fries and toast.

Ben was an older fellow with a lot of experience in business. He went straight to the heart of the matter.

"Tell me what the business is. I like the idea of the book, but that's just the beginning. What the business behind the book."

"There's obviously the speaking and media interviews that go with a successful book, but the real business is in helping young adults start their own businesses.

"Most businesses can be started with a small amount of capital. With my experience in Rotary, my thought is to develop a capital fund that loans money to young adults. The amounts are small; anywhere from a few hundred to three or four thousand. And we team up with local service clubs and business owners.

"The service clubs are support networks for the fledgling business owners, and local business owners help to mentor. I'd like to work at duplicating what the Amish have done.

"Did you know their numbers are almost the exact opposite, when it comes to business success, of everyone else? In the U.S. and Canada, less than five percent of businesses survive past the first five years. In Amish communities, less than five percent of businesses fail. I want to help communities do the same thing for themselves.”

Our food arrived, and Ben looked at the papers I’d handed him.

“Hmmm… Let’s take some time to eat, and let me read this through.”

It only took about twenty minutes for us to eat our meals, and for Ben to read through the plan. Those twenty minutes felt much, much longer.

“I like it.

“I could see the potential by the time I was finished the executive summary. The rest fills in detail, and shows a real business case for what you’re doing.

“You’ve done a lot of good work here.”

“Thank you. That means a lot.”

“You have good material here, and you’ve already published several books. This is something I’m interested in supporting.”

“Wow. That’s cool. Thank you, Ben.”

We talked a while longer about what was needed to get the book published, what Kickstarter is and how it works, and what Ben expected in terms of oversight for the project. Then he asked me about going to the bible study the next day.

"Are you coming to the bible study tomorrow evening?"

I answered as we were standing and putting on our coats. "I'd like to but the van to First Christian leaves at five thirty, and that's my only way to get there. Plus I still have to think about whether Maria is going to be there or not."

"Don't worry about a ride. I'll gladly take you out there after the study. As for Maria, she wasn't there last week, and she hasn't been attending the study lately. Besides, I'm inviting you to be there. I think it's good for you, and for the group."

"Thank you, Ben. I appreciate that. And as long as I have a ride out to First Christian, I can go to the study."

Ben shook my hand and said, "Good. Then we'll see you tomorrow night."

"Yes, sir" I said cheerfully.

When I left the restaurant I was practically walking on air. Having another successful business owner praise what I've done reassured me that I was on the right track. My self-esteem had taken a heavy beating over the last three years, so it's good to know I'm not completely nuts or off my rocker.

Day 81 – Wednesday, 30 Jan – Disappointed, Hurt, Angry, Betrayed

The bible study started at seven. The routine for a Wednesday evening was to wait for the van to First Christian, and then spend the evening at that church. So instead of being at the courthouse for five thirty, I went to the youth center.

Pastor Cook was already there. I pitched in to help arrange the room.

"Hi, Conrad. Are you here for the study?"

Now, Pastor Cook and I had already talked about me attending the bible study. He was concerned that Maria wanted to attend the study, but wouldn't with me there. My perspective was that I was attending the church, and had been invited to attend the study by Ben Fields. This was to prove a contentious issue.

"Yes. I am. Ben and I were talking last night, and he invited me to come."

"Have you thought about what happens if Maria comes in?"

"Stan, I can only take responsibility for myself. If Maria comes, that's great. Maybe it even opens a door for us to start talking; I don't know. But there's no reason for me to stop being here just because Maria *might* show up.

"Ben told me Maria has not been coming to the study, so I'm not expecting there to be an issue." I confess I was a little edgy with Stan (Pastor Pear).

"I thought the order of protection prevented you from being in the same place as Maria."

"No, that isn't what it says. For starters, it only says to refrain from doing certain things. It's only the insane court system that has chosen to reinterpret refrain as meaning prohibited.

"In the case of meeting Maria somewhere around town, the only requirement in the order is that I don't approach her. I don't have to leave, and neither does she. We're just not supposed to talk to each other."

"That would be pretty difficult in a bible study, don't you think?"

"Yes, Stan, I do, but what do you want me to do about it?" I was letting my anger show at this point, and my voice was raised. "I'm attending this church; I'm part of the congregation. Are you telling me not to come to the bible study because someone who is not attending this church, and is not part of the congregation, wants to come? In fact, if Maria attends church at all, it's at Immaculate Conception, and you know that."

"No, no. I'm not telling you to not come. I just think you should give it some thought, that's all."

We went on arranging the room for a few minutes before he spoke again.

"How are you getting out to PADS this evening? It's at First Christian tonight, isn't it?"

"Yes, it is. Ben said he would give me a ride.

"Last night, when he asked me to come, I said I couldn't unless I had a ride afterward. He said not to worry, that he would give me a ride. So, here I am."

That ended the conversation between us for a while. Other people started arriving, and there was general conversation. There was always coffee and some sort of snack laid on for the study. People stand around chatting until Stan asks everyone to take and seat so the study can start.

The youth centre is a large, open room. There's a stage at one end with an area in front that gets filled with chairs for events and church services. Then there's a small conversation pit on one side of the room, and the rest of the area is taken up with bar-height tables and a galley kitchen.

I was standing at one of the tall tables speaking with another member of the study group when Maria arrived. She had stepped far enough inside for the door to close when she saw me. I nodded to her, and she walked back out the door.

Before the door had completely closed, Pastor Cook was at the table talking at me in a clearly angry tone. The color had risen in his cheeks, and he was almost growling when he said, "What are you going to do about this?"

I was a little stunned by his vehemence. "What do you want me to do about it? I can't make her stay."

Stan continued in a heated tone, "You know she wants to come to the bible study, and you know she won't stay as long as you're here. This is not the place to try and work out your differences."

My voice was clear and definite by this point. I wasn't quite angry, but I was offended, and refused to be put onto the defensive. This reminded me a lot of being in the high school play, only I wasn't hurting anyone this time. This time, I was behaving responsibly. I had considered my options, had been given an opportunity and means to attend the study, and decided to attend.

"Stan, I'm not here to try and work things out with Maria. I'm here because I was invited to be here by a member of the congregation."

"But you told me you were here hoping to talk with Maria," he claimed.

"Yes, I've probably said something like that. Is that why I'm here? No. If Maria comes, and we're able to talk, that's a good thing, but it isn't why I'm here, Stan. I'm here because I'm homeless, and have nobody to lean on. I'm hoping that being here, and being part of this congregation, helps me get through the situation I'm in."

That seemed to take a bit of the wind out of Stan's sails. He was, after all, a pastor, and growling at someone during the time for a bible study wasn't what he wanted to be doing.

"Well, okay. As long as that's not the reason for you being here.

"I still think you should give more thought to whether this is the right thing for you to be doing. Maria has been coming to the study for a long time."

"Okay. But Ben tells me Maria has not been coming to the study lately. That's why I felt safe in coming. I know she attended occasionally while we were married, and I came with her a few times, but, again, Ben told me she hasn't been coming lately. So as long as I have a ride out to First Christian, I'm fine with being here."

Stan and I had already talked about this a couple of times, and I had thought it settled. Having to defend myself for accepting an invitation to the bible study was unsettling. I thought this conversation would settle the issue, but it didn't. It would be settled soon.

Day 82 – Thursday, 31 Jan – Disappointed and Misunderstood

When Matthew Parks and I first met, I made a joke about knowing I'm the center of the universe because I wrote the memo that says so. He quoted that from his notes today, and accused me of not taking any responsibility for what has happened between Maria and me.

The conversation wasn't pleasant. It was also this conversation that motivated me to begin recording our sessions. In fact, because I felt Matthew had grossly misinterpreted my joke, I told him that I would be recording future sessions as a way of having an impartial, objective record of the sessions. I even offered to provide him with copies of the sound file from each session.

Here was I, seeking the help that I had tried to get for three years with Maria and the kids, being told that I'm denying my responsibility. That was hard to take. It wasn't made any better by knowing the courts would give a negative interpretation to my quitting the sessions, that Matthew had tremendous power to complicate my life, or that it came on the heels of a pastor berating me for attending a bible study.

The injustice hurt, and it made me want to fight even harder. We were in a small town where everybody knew Maria, and liked her. She took care of everybody's parents or grandparents because she was the nurse for the cardiologist in town. And let's face it... Maria was an attractive, friendly woman who also happens to have been a widow with three children. I was an outsider, and a hard man with anger issues. It's easy to understand how people were more inclined toward the widow who had lived in town for twenty years.

That doesn't make it hurt less, and it doesn't make them right. It actually makes it more wrong for people, like Matthew, who are supposed to strive to remain objective. We are all inclined to interpret things in the way that best suits us, I know. But one thing I've learned is that we have to be on guard against doing this.

You might think someone doesn't speak to you because they don't like you. The truth might be that they're intimidated by you, are in awe of some ability you have, or have simply been taught that they shouldn't speak unless spoken to. The most important thing we can do in relationships is ask questions, give honest answers, and accept the answers we get.

Day 84 – Saturday, 2 Feb – Satisfied, Slightly Timid, and Sad

The first draft of the Kickstarter plan was finished today. It's very satisfying to have this done because it means I'm making real progress toward achieving the goal of publishing Getting Happy...when you wish you were dead. At the same time, I'm a little timid and self-conscious because I'll be asking people to support a project when I'm really about as low as I've ever been.

I'm homeless, have an order of protection against me, have been arrested, and have been committed to a psychiatric facility. My business had ceased to exist, I was being divorced, and a lot of people were telling me I was no good. That's a far cry from coming home with six new clients, and looking forward to a quarter million dollars in first year billings.

Today was 84 days. In less than three months, I had gone from the pinnacle of my business success to being the dregs of society. Today, I feel myself standing at the bottom of a deep, barren, lonely canyon.

With a first draft of the Kickstarter plan finished, encouragement from Ben Fields, and daily support from PADS volunteers, I also feel relief. I can finally see a path that just might lead me up and out of the canyon. I feel encouraged because I know it is my choice to keep working, to keep trying, to want to find a success.

There are a lot of folks at PADS who are being very supportive. They consistently encourage me to keep working on the project, and I trust God to help me make this a book that touches people's lives.

I'm also a little sad. This is the kind of thing I really wanted to do with Maria and the kids. I love them, and they have so much to share because they've lost their dad, plus Maria and I have very similar childhoods. I wish we could be together for this.

Day 86 – Monday, 4 Feb – Encouraged and Lucky

I had an appointment with Dr. Cosmé Lozano today.

We got off to a very rocky start when we first met at Silver Cross Hospital, but we have both turned out to be very different from what was expected.

"Conrad." Cosmé was standing in the doorway. "Would you like to come in?"

We walked down the hall, turned left, and went all the way to the back of the office. Cosmé's office was a windowless room, well furnished with the memorabilia of vacations, his children, and his practice. It was a surprisingly comfortable room.

"How are you today?" hc asked as he settled behind his desk.

I didn't sit down. He had comfortable chairs in his office, but I've always felt a physical disconnection when sitting across a desk from someone. Even my own office had been arranged so the desk was sideways to where people sat. That way I could use the desk, but there was no barrier between us.

So in Cosmé's office, I leaned against a table at

the side of his office.

"I'm okay. I got the first draft of a Kickstarter plan done. That feels good.

"I showed my business plan to Ben Fields. He's a successful, now semi-retired, business owner. He like it, and said he can easily see the potential in what I'm trying to do. That makes me feel very good. It's nice to have outside validation.

I took a deep breath and let it out in a sigh. "But I do have a specific concern I'd like to talk to you about. Other stuff is happening, too, like Maria and I getting divorced, but we can come back to that."

"What's your concern?"

"Well, as you know, Maria and I are getting divorced." He nodded as I continued. "I also got a letter recently telling me I'm no longer covered by her health benefits. So that means I don't have any insurance, and I have to tell you straight that I don't have any income.

"We Care, the local food bank, gave me the transit fare to get here today, and I don't have any way to even pay the twenty dollar co-pay for each visit. So I don't have any way to keep seeing you."

Cosmé took me seriously. He stopped making notes, sat back in his chair and talked to me.

"Well, you already know I'm fairly successful at

what I do. I have a good practice, and I make quite a bit of money. That allows me the freedom to see who I want to see, and do what I want to do." I nodded and muttered agreement.

"Conrad, if you're willing to keep doing the work you're doing... As long as you keep making the progress I've already seen, then I'm willing to see you. You don't have to pay anything."

When the appointment was over, he walked out with me. He made a point of telling his receptionist that he would continue seeing me, and that I was not to be charged anything for future visits. He would take care of the costs.

This was a big deal for me. Here was a doctor, a psychiatrist no less, who was setting aside everything to help me.

As it happened, I wouldn't see Dr. Cosmé Lozano again. We would exchange e-mails, and eventually lose contact completely, but this recognition and acknowledgement was a key element in my being able to keep moving forward.

Day 88 – Wednesday, 6 Feb – Hurt, Angry and Depressed

"Dear Conrad,

"I spoke with Maria regarding Wednesday night bible study. She would like to attend bible study on Wednesday's but has determined at this time it is not healthy to attend if you are attending. So, she will come tonight, but if you are already there she will leave and she is ok with doing this.

"As we talked last week, I have been praying about this situation and thought a solution was at hand because of PADS transportation being provided at 6:00 PM. But now someone has recently been asked by you to provide a ride to First Christian following tonight's study.

"Please pray for God's direction regarding Wednesday night study. As your Pastor, I am blessed when anyone desires to read and study God's Word so I hope you can appreciate the conflicting position this place me. I have expressed to you the full picture regarding the longevity of attendance and strained relationship between you and Maria. I understand both positions and each of your actions. Maria has worked through this from the stand point if you are there, she will leave.

"What are thoughts?

"Pastor Stan Pear, Lead Pastor, Living Water Church of the Nazarene."

This e-mail arrived at 12:19 pm today. It's fair to say I found it upsetting. That might even be a wee bit of an understatement.

The person asked to provide a ride was Ben Fields. The same person who provided a ride for the last two weeks, and who invited me to keep attending the study.

As you might imagine, my reply to Stan was to accede to his request. I chose to stop attending the bible study, and to stop attending Stan's church. It was a little hard to accept someone as "your Pastor" while he was also clearly siding against you. It was even harder to let go of the support of a congregation when I was homeless, had no family, and it meant losing Ben Fields' support for the book project.

Ben was part of the leadership for the congregation. It seemed unreasonable to ask him for continued help and support when his pastor was taking support away. So I never pushed him or even tried to stay in touch.

Losing a relationship always hurts, even when the relationship is toxic. But the only good thing to do with a toxic relationship is end it.

Day 90 – Friday, 8 Feb – Intrigued and Validated

I started reading William Glasser's *Reality Therapy in Action*. Matthew Parks told me about him, and his approach seems to line up with mine.

I've been using the motto "Cranium Ex Rectum" for years and people seem to genuinely like it. Yes, I'm telling people to pull their heads out of their arses, but I also do it with genuine compassion mixed with just enough sternness to get attention. So I very much like Dr. Glasser's approach of taking responsibility for what I choose to feel.

Sometimes that's hard just because my emotions are swinging between great big arcs and zigzags.

When I start blaming Maria I also start thinking about how unfair all of this is. Then I pull back from blaming and try to only deal with the things I've said and done. That's hard, and a little frustrating, but it draws out softer emotions.

The last thing I want is to ever hate Maria or even get revenge, but sometimes that's how I feel. We might never be together again, yet it's good to know I'm okay for wishing her well and wanting the best for all of us.

Maybe part of what's needed is some time and distance from the situation. The idea that "time heals all wounds" is crap, but it does take time for a wound to heal enough that touching it stops being agony.

Day 92 – Sunday, 10 Feb – Sad, Wanting to Quit

I cried over Maria today. I keep praying to have her back, but I'm afraid she is lost to me.

Dr. Glasser makes the point that we often do things we know are wrong for us – even though it seems like the best choice at the time. I've certainly done that, and I'm experiencing it with Maria as we go through this divorce. It really hurts that she had me arrested for telling her I love her and want to work things out, and even more to hear her lying in court. Then add on being in PADS, thinking I've lost her for good, and feeling generally bummed, I guess it's no surprise I'm crying for losing her.

The last time I remember crying was a few days after the car accident in 1994.

September 23, 1994. I was on debarkation leave because my military unit was heading for The Former Republic of Yugoslavia. We had two weeks leave, and I was heading home to say goodbye to my parents.

We hadn't spoken in a long time. I figured it would be good to say goodbye because my plan was to never return.

I was distracted, and was driving a road I had driven thousands of times while going to high school. It's proper name is Ridge Road, but everyone calls it Snake Road. It follows an escarpment going left, right, up and down.

I was driving fast. The last time I looked at the speedometer I was doing 84 kph – that's about 52 mph.

That glance at the speedometer came seconds after seeing a yellow, diamond shaped sign warning me of a hairpin turn. It suggested slowing to 20 kph. As luck would have it, rain had just started to fall.

I remember the sound of the car hitting something. Later, my warrant officer would explain the car hit a tree right at the driver's door. It was bent into a horseshoe shape.

It took 10 ½ hours of surgery to put me back together.

The phone call my parents received was "Your son is in surgery, and we don't expect him to come out."

My mother took that call. She decided to wait until my father got home from work rather than call him because, as she explained to me, "there was nothing he could do anyway, so it made no sense to bother him at work."

There are a lot of things I remember from that

experience.

Waking up in the car being unable to breathe. Waking up during surgery to see a masked man with his fingers in the side of my chest and a plastic tube in his other hand. Waking up in ICU and scaring the daylights out a nurse.

Six days after the accident, I was alone in a hospital room. A nurse and orderly had just been there to see if I could stand and walk. It was after they left that I was lying in bed and cried.

It was brief. I think I was crying partly because I was glad to be alive, and partly because I wished I wasn't.

When I cried over losing Maria, it was partly because I was losing another family – her and the kids. It was also sorrow over having made so many bad choices and having to live with the consequences.

Day 96 – Thursday, 14 Feb – Depressed, Resigned, and a bit Suicidal

I had an appointment with Matthew Parks today. Maybe it was a good thing.

It's Valentine's Day, so of course I'm missing Maria even more today. I tell Matthew I'm pretty much resigned to giving Maria the divorce. It's scheduled for next Tuesday – the 19th – and there's really not much I can do about it. But inside I'm really just lost. I wish I could just go stick my head in the river and drown (although I don't tell him that).

I'm so lost in my head that after I leave Matthew's office, I hatch a hare-brained, last-ditch effort at getting Maria to change direction. After all, it's Valentine's Day, right? I'm not resigned to being divorced. I want to be with my wife and the kids.

So I criss-cross town getting the "magic charms" that will win Maria back to me.

My first stop is a mile south from Matthew's office to get a dark chocolate, 70% cocoa bar. Then it's a walk a mile north to get a Valentine's Day card from the grocery store. (Which is four blocks east from Matthew's office.) Then it's south again to meet with Dan Peterson at We Care. (Yep, that's just two blocks west from where I bought the chocolate bar.)

I had asked Dan to meet me so I could talk to him about my phenomenal plan for winning Maria. Dan had doubts. Dan expressed his doubts. I didn't listen. In fact, I had convinced myself that I was doing what Maria "really" wanted. Call me Captain Obvious, but just because you know you're making a choice doesn't mean you're making the right, best, or even rational choice.

I put the chocolate bar and card into a Ziploc baggie, walked north again to where Maria worked, and put the "presents" on the windshield of her car.

This would either finally break through, or be the last door closing.

Day 97 – Friday, 15 Feb – Chagrined and Disappointed

The last door is closed between Maria and me.

The police showed up at the library to arrest me because she filed a complaint after Valentine's Day.

Day 98 – Tuesday, 16 Feb

"Hall. Time for court."

The shackles go on my wrists and ankles.

William Paternost is in the courtroom when I arrive.

"This is probably going to be straightforward. Since this is the second violation of the order of protection, the state's attorney is entitled to ask for a psych evaluation and he likely will."

"What does that mean?" I ask.

"You remain in custody until the evaluation is done, and the results arrive at the state's attorney's office. Once they have the results, we schedule another hearing to determine whether you can be released on bail. So there probably won't be anything for you to say or do today."

Then he walked away; assembly line law enforcement.

The state's attorney asked for a psych evaluation.

I felt like a door stop. I was just something to be moved from place to place, and used to serve the purposes of other people. Giving up all hope for justice settled into me between last night and today. It is truly not personal for anyone involved; except for Maria and me. They have no interest in anything beyond doing their jobs.

Day 101 – Tuesday, 19 Feb – Belittled, Angry and Hateful

Today is the day for Maria and me to be divorced. I'm still in jail, so I am paraded before a court full of people in chains (literally bound with ankle and wrist shackles). It's the embarrassing result of a bad choice.

Maria commits perjury when I ask her whether she has a philosophy of "I'll always tell you the truth, just not always the whole truth." She answer no, that she does not have such a philosophy. Today I hate Maria for lying.

There was no real need to ask her anything. Her lawyer had questioned her, and then me, so pretty much everything was covered. I knew what was about to happen, but I wanted to ask her that one question.

I wanted to know whether she would tell the truth.

I gave up trying at that point. The judge has been the same person throughout this whole process. I've said it in court several times that he is clearly biased, has a relationship with Maria through her work, and that he is incapable of rendering a just verdict. Instead of making anyone upset, that approach only gets people to tell me that I won't win by offending the judge.

The judge grants Maria a divorce, and I go back to jail and waiting for the psych evaluation.

Day 110 - Thursday, 28 Feb

The evaluator arrives today. I'm escorted from my cell to a visitor room, and left alone with the evaluator.

"Hello, Mr. Hall. Do you know why I'm here?" Not even an introduction; just straight into the assembly line practice.

"Yes. You're here to dot i's and cross t's."

"I'm sorry? What does that mean?"

"It means you're here to do a job. You have a job to do. You're going to do it, and it doesn't matter whether anything about it is true or accurate."

You might be thinking at this point that I don't learn very well. Wouldn't it be better to play along? To tell people what they want to hear? I think telling people what they want to hear is just fine, as long as they want to hear the truth. I think most people do want to hear the truth, and they're in jobs where they rarely hear it; especially in court related situations. This time, it worked out in my favor to be a little shocking.

"That's not really true," she said calmly. "Yes, I have a job to do, but that doesn't mean I just want to fill in a form and be done. What I'd like to do is talk to you about your situation and find out how you feel about it. Is that okay?"

"Okay. Let's talk."

The visitor's room is divided down the middle by Plexiglas and steel supports. There are half a dozen stools on each side, and you normally talk to each other through a telephone setup. In this case, the evaluator was in the same section of the room as me, and I was handcuffed.

The stools are all steel, there's a small ledge at each visiting station, and a concrete ledge at the end of the room. I'm a restless person, always fidgeting and moving, so I kept moving from one stool to another and to the concrete ledge as we talked.

"Alright. I'm here because you've violated an order of protection twice. Would you like to tell me why you did that?"

"Sure.

"First, I didn't actually violate the order." Seeing her eyebrows come up, I quickly followed that claim with an explanation. "I know the court says I did, and I agree that I did everything they say I did. But nothing I did violated the order of protection.

"You see, the order says, in big, bold letters, that I am to *refrain* from doing a whole list of things. My position is that I can't violate an order that says to *refrain*. If it said *prohibited* or *forbidden* then I would agree that I had violated the order, but it doesn't say that. And I do not accept that this court decides to reinterpret the English language."

"So you don't think you've done anything wrong?"

"No, I didn't say that. In fact, there are lots of things I've done wrong, and I've made lots of mistakes. I'm facing up to those mistakes, and doing what I can to either fix them or avoid making them again.

"What I am saying is that yes, I did what they say I did, but no, it doesn't violate the concept of refraining from doing those things. I kept myself from contacting Maria as much as I could, and the finally gave in to the desire to reconcile with my wife. Do you understand?

"Yes, I do. That's an unusual position."

"Well, you'll find I'm an unusual guy," I said with a smile and chuckle. "I try very hard to get rid of my illusions, and face each situation as honestly as I can. Of course, that sometimes creates difficulty when dealing with other people."

"That's admirable," she said as she glanced down at her notes.

"So can you tell me why you contacted your wife when the order of protection said you shouldn't?"

"Yes.

"I wanted to work things out. Maria has said and done a lot of things that aren't true during this whole process, and we both have to live with that. I wanted to give her every opportunity to change direction, tell the truth, and work toward making a happy, healthy marriage. I love her, and I love the kids. I didn't want to lose them.

"I contacted her precisely because the order of protection says to *refrain* from contacting her. It does not say I'm *prohibited*. So I thought it through, I chose what I thought to be the least offensive, most honest way of communicating with her, and then reached out to my wife.

"And just to make sure the point is clear: The order says *refrain* precisely because it isn't allowed to say *prohibited*. So what's truly galling about this situation is that it's happening because the whole system chooses to behave as though they are allowed to say *prohibited*."

She didn't say anything to that, but she paused for a bit. She seemed to be thinking about what I had said.

"And what about now? How do you feel about your wife now?"

"Well, it's a different situation now. Do I love her? Yes. Would I like to be with her and the kids? Hmmm... Mostly.

"The fact is that we were divorced last week. So that's it, the marriage is over. Maria has followed this process to a conclusion. A divorce is not something you can undo.

"And before you say it, yes, we could get back together and work things out. Sure. Anything is possible. But in this case, that would not be possible for me. Maria has chosen divorce, and now all of us - her, me, and the kids - have to live with that."

"So, if you're released, you're saying you wouldn't try to contact your wife?"

"Former-wife, actually. And no, I'm not saying that. I don't see any point in answering the question.

"Think about it. I'm in jail, and I want to get out. The only way to do that is convince you I'm not going to contact Maria; that I pose no threat to her. So whether it's the truth or not, I'm going to say 'No ma'am. There's no way I would try to contact Maria.'

"No matter what I say, you can't trust the answer to that question.

"In fact, there's no way for you, or anyone else, to be sure of what I intend or don't intend. Do you want to hear me say it? No, I'm not going to contact Maria. The marriage is over, so there's no point to contacting her.

"Yes, there's still the property settlement to be worked out. That means we'll see each other in court, and that's it. I need to put my time and energy into figuring out where I go from here. What do I do? What do I want to do? Maria has chosen her future, and now I have to start looking after mine."

"You've been doing a lot of thinking about this, haven't you?"

I stopped to look at her with a "is that rhetorical?" look on my face. Then I shrugged and raised my hands saying "Not much else to do around here, is there?"

She smiled slightly and nodded.

"You've told me what you're going to do. Can you tell me how you feel toward your ex-wife?"

"Now that's a harder question.

"How I feel changes from hour to hour. Sometimes I'm angry and feel betrayed, other times I try to make allowance for her, and sometimes I'm just depressed.

"If you're asking whether I hate her, the answer is sometimes. Like I said, how I feel is all over the map, but here's the thing: What matters to me is moving forward with my life.

"I can't do that in jail. And I can't move forward if I keep trying to make things different between Maria and me. The only person I can control is me. Maria has made her position clear, and I have to accept it. So moving forward means leaving her and the kids behind.

"Do I like that? No.

"Am I going to do it anyway? Yes. My health and well-being are more important to me than any relationship."

Her voice was calm and genuine as she wrapped things up. "Well, Mr. Hall, you've made a lot of good points."

She made a few notes, and closed the file folder. "Now, I don't make the final decision, but I don't think you pose a threat to your wife."

Day 115 – Tuesday, 5 Mar – Free, Happy and a little Concerned

William Paternost, the public defender, came to the jail yesterday to prepare for today's hearing. It was an interesting conversation.

"Hi, Mr. Hall. How would you like to proceed tomorrow?"

"I beg your pardon? What do mean 'How do I want to proceed?'

"Isn't that why you're here? To tell me how it works?"

William was happy and chipper, decked out in casual pants, a nice shirt, and shiny leather jacket. This was clearly a pleasant occasion for him.

"Okay. I'd be happy to." William rubbed his hands together and leaned forward a little in excitement.

"I'm pretty sure I can work out a plea bargain for you. You didn't do anything violent, there's no history of violence, and you didn't even really try to contact Maria. You just left some stuff on the windshield of her car."

"Really? And how do you know that?" I interrupted.

"They have video evidence," he said in surprise.

"And you've seen this video evidence?"

"No, but they wouldn't say they have it if they didn't," he said with assurance.

"Right. Because the police and state's attorney would never lie." My voice was rich with sarcasm.

"But let's say this video evidence does exist. If you haven't seen it, how do you know it shows me leaving something on Maria's car? How do you know that the person in video is even identifiable?"

"Like I said, they wouldn't be saying they have evidence if it wasn't good enough to stand up in court," he replied curtly. "So I'm guessing you want to plead not guilty?"

"Since it's impossible for me to be guilty, yes, I intend to plead not guilty."

"What do you mean it's not possible for you to be guilty?

"Well, the order says to refrain, right? That word is in big, bold letters on the order. So how can I violate an order that tells me to refrain from doing something? I did refrain. I refrained as best I could under the circumstances, then I reached out to my wife to try and work things out."

"You're right. The order says refrain, but the court interprets that as meaning prohibited," he said with some heat in his voice. William didn't seem to be having as much fun now that someone was actively participating, and keeping him from playing out his part.

"Okay. Except you're not allowed to do that. You can't decide that, in this building, a word has one meaning for the rest of the world but it's going to have a different meaning when you're here. That's ridiculous. You don't get to redefine the English language just because it suits you."

William was definitely displeased at this point. His brow was furrowed, his voice had hardened, and his hands had closed into fists resting on his thighs. At least he was still sitting down.

"Okay. That takes care of the first charge of violating the order. What about the second violation?"

"What do you mean? It's still the same order. You can't violate something that tells you to refrain."

"Okay, you're right, but didn't you walk through the parking lot at Maria's place of work?"

"Even if I did, so what? How does that make a difference?"

William opened a file folder and took out a copy of the order of protection.

"You're right that the order says to refrain on the first page. But on the second page, it specifies that you are prohibited from going to several places including Maria's place of work."

He handed me the pages to let me read. That took a few seconds.

"Okay. I get it, and I see two problems.

"First, it says I'm not allowed to go to these places when they are there. So, for example, I could go to the high school for a football game in the evening or a weekend because there's no reason to expect Maria or the kids would be there.

"In this case, let's call it a wash. If I did was I'm accused of, then clearly Maria was in the building. Stuff was left on the windshield of her car. But that doesn't mean I went to her place of work. The parking lot is used by a couple of dozen businesses in the same building. And my experience is that Maria always parks in the south parking lot. But her 'place of work' is on the north side of the building. So even if I put stuff on her car, I still didn't go to her place of work."

With some exasperation, I asked "Isn't this what you're supposed to doing? I mean, you're the lawyer, aren't you supposed to be working out how to defend me? It seems more like you're trying to figure out how to make the prosecutor's job easy."

As you can imagine, William didn't appreciate that very much.

"You're not going to get very far with that line here. The state's attorney is not going to let you walk on both charges. You're going to have to take some kind of plea bargain."

"Wow. That really sucks, doesn't it?"

"It's not fun, I agree, but it was you, after all, who violated the order twice."

"Aha. Right. So what am I supposed to do next?"

William visibly calmed down since I seemed to be doing what was expected of me.

"Well, your psych evaluation came back. It says you're a low risk. That's good. You've never been in trouble before... "William was reading notes from his file folder."There's no history of violence, you never actually tried to contact Maria directly... You did have a pastor contact her for you... You've been seeing a counsellor... Are you still seeing the counsellor at Batterdrum Health?"

"Yes."

"Good. You've only ever said you love her and want to work things out...

"Alright. I can probably get the state's attorney to drop one of the charges. You plead guilty to the other charge, and I'll get the state's attorney to agree to time served. You'll have to agree to keep seeing the counsellor, and he might require you to attend a diversion program. Maybe I can get him to waive that if you agree to keep seeing the counsellor at Batterdrum Health."

"Well, I'm going to keep seeing Matthew no matter what the judge says. I'm doing that for me and my improvement. If it works in my favor, that's great."

"Okay. Leave this with me, and I'll touch base with you tomorrow before the hearing."

Today, William spoke to me in the courtroom. As usual, my hands and feet were shackled together and I was sitting where a jury would otherwise be seated.

He spoke softly. "The state's attorney has agreed to proceed on only one charge. You'll receive a non-reporting, twelve month discharge, you agree to keep seeing your counsellor, and you're out of jail today."

"What is a non-reporting, twelve month discharge?"

"It basically means you agree to abide by the order of protection, and not break any other laws. You don't report to anyone, you just agree to behave for twelve months."

"And if I don't agree to this?"

"Then you go back to jail until we can schedule a trial," he said with a testy edge to his voice.

"How long does that take?"

"It's hard to say. It will be at least three months, and could be six or seven. That's up to the state's attorney and his schedule. But if you take the plea bargain, you can be out of jail this afternoon. What do you want to do?"

"Well, I guess I'll take the plea bargain."

And that was it. I pled guilty, and was released from jail.

I was definitely happy to be free after 19 days in jail. It may seem a short time for a vacation, or a holiday, but jail is a slow place. Every day feels like two. And I've been away from the book project all that time. Do I still want to work on it? Every day has been focused on introspection and self-analysis, with everything else pushed to the side.

I'm divorced, living in PADS, my business has disintegrated, and there are no employment prospects for me in this small town. What do I really want to do?

Day 117 – Thursday, 7 Mar – Defeated but Resolute

I set up my mail to be forwarded from the house to General Delivery today. It was pretty embarrassing at the post office, but Linda (the lady most often at the counter) was very nice and helped me get it done right. It's sort of the end of my last hope that Maria and I might be reconciled, but it also means I'm definitely moving forward. I want people – and my mail – to find me.

On the bright side, Mike Lord invited me to his house this morning. He knows I'm alone and missing Maria, so he invited me over for tea and conversation. Mike is one of the volunteers at PADS. He has a quaint, one bedroom apartment above a funeral home. It's good to have someone to talk with.

Day 122 – Tuesday, 12 Mar – Defeated and Alone

I'm feeling defeated. A week since getting out of jail and I can't seem to get my legs back under me, or my mind back onto the book. The forced idleness of jail has settled into my bones.

Even worse is that I'm alone. My wife and family are gone.

I met with Matthew Parks today, and I was all over the map. Sometimes talking to him is such an exercise in being sure he cannot misinterpret what I'm saying that it's hard to get any value from talking to him. Plus I'm split over how to feel toward Maria.

So much of what happened during our marriage is a result of both of us making mistakes. We both needed help and acknowledged that, but we didn't get the help. So we're both wrong, and I don't think we were trying to be mean to each other. But now Maria is telling lies to get what she wants, and that makes me angry. I want us to be together again, but I'm not willing to let what has happened since November just slide.

There's a story in Dr. Glasser's book about a woman who is unhappy with her husband. That triggered a memory about Maria asking me to go to bible study two or three months before all this happened.

When she asked, I was happy. She asked as I was walking past the kitchen. I kept going and went into the bedroom. When I got into the bedroom, I started thinking about her request in terms of all the efforts I had made that she undermined and all the efforts she had made and failed to sustain. I also thought about having told her we were through because of all the pain she had caused.

My attitude was very 'blaming" and I wanted to push her away and hurt her.

Instead of saying yes and making the most of the opportunity, I said no. More specifically, I growled at her and said "The only thing we have left to do together - if it's required - is the immigration interview." Then I walked away.

When I think about it now, I wonder how hard it was for Maria to invite me. I wonder whether it was hard for her to speak up. Whether it was or wasn't, it's certain I shut her down hard.

There's no question in my mind that I was hard on Maria during the last year of our marriage. I was angry and hurt after absorbing two years of abuse. I had given up on our marriage.

That Maria has resorted to lies to achieve her

objective hurts now, but I can't do anything about someone else's choices. It's something I know in my head, and have a hard time taking action on. It's a lot easier to just blame her for doing things that are clearly wrong than it is to focus on the things I could have done better. That's the big trap, isn't it?

I think of times when the kids were fighting; especially Skyler and Skyler. One time Skyler wouldn't give back something of Skyler's, so Skyler hit Skyler. That started a fight that carried all the way into the bedroom where Maria and I were lazing about with the cat and dog. I stepped into the door of the bedroom and called the girls.

"What's going on?" I asked.

"Skyler has my game and won't give it back."

"Well you hit me!"

"Hold on. Hold on. One at a time.

"Skyler, what's the problem?"

"But she hit me," Skyler interrupted.

"Okay. And you'll have your turn in a second. One of you has to go first, right? And all I'm asking Skyler is to explain what happened. Then I'll ask you, okay?" Skyler still wanted to go first, but she accepted the situation.

"Skyler, what happened?"

"Skyler had my game and wouldn't give it back,

so I went in her room and got it."

"Okay. And did you hit your sister?"

"Yes."

"Alright. Skyler, what do you say happened?"

"Well, I wasn't finished with her game, but she didn't have to hit me."

"You're right. Skyler should not have hit you. In fact, she shouldn't even have gone into your room if you didn't want her there. So let's see if we can work this out.

"First, Skyler, do you now have your game back?" I could see something in her hand, but wasn't sure if it was the game.

She held it up for me to see. "Yes."

"Okay. So here's how I see it. Skyler, you had something of Skyler's and didn't return it when asked it that right?"

"Yes." Then I looked at Skyler for an answer.

"Yes."

"And Skyler, you went into your sister's room to get it. When she wouldn't give it back, you hit her, is that right?"

"Yes." Skyler agreed when I glanced at her for an answer.

"So you both did something wrong, and instead

of getting what you wanted, it started a fight. Now we're standing here talking about it." The girls were watching me, wondering what would come next.

"You're sisters, right?" They nodded. "And I know you love each other. You're always doing stuff together, but today you got on each other's nerves.

"So, do you think you can go back to your rooms and work this out without fighting?"

That was all it took; a short conversation to help both sides see what they could have done differently. Looking back, I think I should have hugged both girls, given them a kiss, and told them they were loved, but I didn't. It just didn't occur to me at the time.

When I think about things like this, I wonder what makes it so easy to help someone else solve a problem that I'm not solving for myself. Maria and I were doing the same sort of thing, and I kept reacting with anger instead of trying to find a solution. Or no, it wasn't just anger. I was also blaming Maria for hurting me and then letting that justify the anger instead of looking for a solution.

Ever notice how often we all do that? It's entirely correct to say that Maria did things that even she agreed were wrong, so I feel good about blaming her and being angry. When she "reacts poorly" to my blame and anger, I feel justified in telling her she can fix it all by just correcting what she's doing wrong. And it all ends up in divorce and hurt feelings.

Now, I'm not saying that Maria and I would ever have ended up with a happy, healthy marriage. It's possible that we would have ended up going our separate ways anyway. But I am saying that I could have given her my love instead of anger, listened instead of complaining, and support instead of nagging.

All week - to be honest, for about the last two years - I had been choosing what felt good today instead of what's best for the long haul. I had been wallowing in trying to figure out what I could have done differently, pitying myself for things having gone wrong, and blaming everyone (including myself) for not having made their best effort.

I want different results, so it's time to make a different choice.

Day 124 – Thursday, 14 Mar – Disappointed but Determined

We had a Motion Hearing on the property settlement today. Maria committed perjury again, only this time it was over several questions I put to her. I feel disappointment, and choose to not feel angry. I wish it were different between Maria and me, but I also accept that she's on a course not easily changed now.

The judge wants to see proofs of our claims regarding property, so the case is continued until Thursday, 2 May at 9:30 am. He also orders Maria to surrender files from my office at the house. Those files contain receipts that prove my claims.

I had an appointment with Matthew Parks this afternoon and told him what happened. I also told him about telling the judge I think he is biased, and has judged this case unfairly. The judge's reply was that it's a bad idea to say something like that to him if I expect a favourable verdict. I guess he can't see that this is the very attitude I'm complaining about. What justice is there if it requires kissing up to the judge?

We talked about me wanting to get back together with Maria, and that I don't want to let things slide.

I don't think he understands – or doesn't want to understand – that I expect Maria to own up to the lies she has told precisely because I do love her. How could we ever have a healthy, loving marriage if we're not honest with each other? The thing that really chafes is that I think the only way Maria will admit to having lied is if she's made to do it in court. Could any value ever come from forcing her to admit she lied?

The hardest thing about this situation is the way I keep flipping and flopping. I hate the idea of admitting defeat and am truly sad at failing to build a family with Maria. I try to move forward, and keep falling back into thinking we might work things out.

What I really need is to replace the idea of getting back together with something constructive. After all, nature abhors a vacuum, right?

I told Matthew about my biggest dreams for the book project today. That was a mistake. I could see it in his face. He thinks I'm delusional. Maybe I am. I want to believe my story can help people find their way to getting happy. But maybe I'm just kidding myself.

Day 127 – Sunday, 17 Mar – Distracted, Re-Committed

Part of making a different choice, of being sure I'm not kidding myself, is staying committed to getting work done for the book and Kickstarter campaign. I realised today that I've been thinking about the work, but really doing anything. This has been a stumbling block for most of my life.

I equate thinking about a project, or talking about it, with getting things done. It's a brutal form of self-sabotage. This time, I'm making it different.

Everybody says knowing a problem exists is half the battle. I'm not quite sure that's accurate, but it's dead certain you can't do anything about a problem until you admit it exists. So today I talked to myself about what the problem is, what I want to do differently, and how to go about it.

I re-committed to doing the work, and started getting it done today. I put action with my thoughts and words. I sat down and went through all the notes I have for the book and the Kickstarter campaign to get my mind back into completing both. Part of sorting through everything is trying to form some sort of schedule for myself.

I'm still in PADS, so there is a basic structure of

having to be at each church by six pm, and being out the door each morning by seven am. I spoke with the folks at We Care last week, and decided to volunteer there each Monday, Wednesday and Thursday morning. It feels very good to be doing something constructive with my time, and there's the bonus of being able to have extra food. And I'm seeing Matthew Parks every Tuesday and Friday in the morning.

That gives me every afternoon to be at the library working on the book and Kickstarter project.

Since disagreeing with Pastor Cook, and leaving the congregation, the support from Ben Fields has evaporated. That's disappointing, but it mostly makes sense. Making this work means having to make new relationships and new connections.

I have a blogsite up for the book. I've posted a couple of times, and am working at finding things to write about. It's a little scary to be taking a Cranium Ex Rectum attitude in the posts. It's definitely good to make people sit up and take notice, but risking the negative reactions is a little scary when you don't have any sort of home base.

The post I wrote today was about being happy even though I don't have all the stuff of a normal, stable life. I got thinking yesterday about what it was like after a car accident I had eighteen and half years ago. It was a bad accident.

I was in the army at the time, and on my way to see my parents for the first time in years. My unit was headed overseas, and I had no intention of coming back. The easiest way to commit suicide is picking a fight in a war zone.

Anyway, I was driving along Snake Road. That isn't its real name; just a nickname because the road twists back and forth, and goes up and down an escarpment. It's a road I used to drive all the time when going to high school.

The last time I looked at the speedometer, I was doing eighty-four kilometers an hour (about fifty-two miles per hour). That was just after seeing a yellow warning sign showing a hairpin turn ahead. The sign recommended doing twenty kilometers (fifteen miles) per hour through the turn. It had just started to rain, and the road was slick. I never made it through the turn.

It took ten and a half hours of surgery to put me back together.

I remember getting back to the barracks after leaving the hospital. Everyone was packing because they were leaving the next day. Have you ever seen one of those movies where someone is walking down a hallway and everybody comes out of the rooms to stare at the person? That's what happened to me.

You see, everyone in my unit had been told I was killed in the crash. They didn't know I was alive.

When I showed up in the barracks twelve days later, I looked a lot like a ghost. My clothes hung loosely because I had lost so much weight. I was exhausted from the trip and was dragging my feet, and everyone said I was white as a sheet. Probably not the most encouraging thing to see the night before leaving for overseas duty.

Even though I was tired, weak and in pain, I remember being thankful to be alive. Strange, isn't it? Before the car accident, I had attempted suicide thirty-two times. Some of them came very close to being successful. Then, the one time I succeed in getting myself killed, it's in a car accident when I had absolutely no intention or desire to hurt myself.

Ever since that accident, the colours have been a little more intense, and I've listened better. It wasn't any kind of magic cure, of course. It didn't suddenly turn my life around, or turn me into John Maxwell or Seth Godin. But the experience has certainly stayed with me.

That's what I was thinking about yesterday, and what I wrote about today. My life is far from ideal right now, and I'm still grateful to be alive. Alive, I can make things happen, work toward success, and keep making choices.

In a way, it's the same decision or realization I made on the bridge a couple months ago. Then it was anger that encouraged me to think "No way am

I letting all the bastards I've met in my life win." I'd be lying if I said the anger was all gone, but there's something else with it now. In addition to wanting to prove people wrong, there's a desire to build a happy, healthy, productive life.

Day 129 – Tuesday, 19 Mar – Frustrated

Today was one of my regular appointments with Matthew Parks. It turns out he is reading my blog. After we had a little chit-chat, he asked about the post I wrote yesterday.

"That's an interesting post you wrote yesterday."

"Thank you. I thought it made a good point."

"Yes, but I wonder how you were feeling when you wrote it. You skipped over a lot of stuff, didn't you?"

"What do you mean?"

"Well, we've been talking for a few months, right?" I nodded in agreement. "In that time, you've gone back and forth a lot over Maria and how you feel. Sometimes you're ready to move on, sometimes you want to work things out, you're angry, you love her... It's hard to read your post and understand how it is that you're happy."

"Really." My voice was flat. This was truly annoying. This is the guy who is supposed to be supporting and encouraging my efforts, yet it feels like he takes every opportunity to poke holes.

"So, what? You're telling me that because I'm

experiencing the normal emotional fluctuations of being betrayed, divorced, arrested, homeless, having a business disintegrate, and feeling like everyone is on my former-wife's side and against me, I can't possibly find any happiness in the day? What kind of crap is that?"

"You said it yourself, didn't you? How can you find be happy when you feel all that weighing you down?"

I laughed without mirth and replied, "Isn't that what you're supposed to be telling me? How to find a way to be happy?"

Matthew smirked. "I'm more interested in making sure you're being real with yourself, and not living in a delusion."

"Right. And, of course, if I can't be happy every minute of the day... if I'm not consistently happy without ever having thoughts of wanting to get even, or wanting to fix things, or whatever... I just can't be happy if I'm still having negative thoughts, is that it?"

"No, I'm not saying that. It just seems odd that you're dreaming of success with a book when you're homeless, and you're talking about being happy when even you say your emotions are all over the board. I wonder if you aren't kidding yourself just a little."

Talking with Matthew is often more frustrating than it is helpful.

Day 130 – Wednesday, 20 Mar – Satisfied, Happy, Ambitious

Getting Happy… when you wish you were dead gelled in my mind today. I finally understand how I'll put it together so it makes sense and people will – I hope – enjoy reading it.

I'll use this period of my life, and include flashbacks to my childhood. It really sank in today that suicide is about feeling disconnected and ineffective. So what if people can read this and see that, even when you're feeling hopelessly bad, there is still an opportunity to choose. There have been lots of days when choosing is the last thing I wanted to do, and there are likely to be more in the future. It isn't fun, but it's okay. Taking a day off - maybe a few days off - is sometimes what you need to do, I know. And then you come back, make some more choices, and get some more work done.

This is the hardest book I'll ever write. It's my story, and it hurts to remember everything well enough to write it down. Okay. But that's what I need to do for my healing and progress. And who knows, maybe it helps just one person to choose getting happy when they're wishing to be dead.

I also finally let Maria go. Thinking about her

and what she has done to me only gives away control of my life. It's time to set that memory aside and focus on my forward progress. It's time to write the book.

Today I am happy. There are sure to be up days and down days, achievements and disappointments, but I've learned how to start the day with gratitude and choose how I respond. I'm looking forward to sharing Getting Happy...when you wish you were dead.

Day 132 – Friday, 22 Mar – Productive and Challenged

I started laying out this outline today. I got a lot of the pieces in place, and need to read through my journal to fill in gaps. I'll also ask people like Matthew and Millie to help me fill things in.

I've always known this would be the most difficult manuscript for me to write. This is, I guess, the real start of it. It's one thing to put down the dates and what happened, but making this outline means attaching emotions to each day and event. That's a hard thing to do.

Especially after meeting with Matthew Parks today. He brought up my biggest dream for Getting Happy and asked whether I'm being at all realistic. That really pissed me off. It doesn't seem to matter that I have a Have To Hit goal, a This Is Great goal, and a Dance On The Ceiling goal. He only cares that the Dance On The Ceiling goal doesn't seem realistic. Well, duh, but it isn't supposed to seem realistic – neither is dancing on the ceiling!

Day 133 – Saturday, 23 Mar – Excited and Fearful

All the events are listed in this timeline. It's going to be the foundation structure for *Getting Happy...when you wish you were dead*. So I'm very happy about having this done. Now I have to go back through it and start attaching emotions to the events.

I wrote in my journal today: "It has always been amazing to me that people like Matthew Parks ask me to do incredibly difficult things – such as distance myself from an experience as I'm doing with this timeline. Then they get angry when I achieve what they thought I could not do."

On the bright side, getting the timeline done meant Matthew bought me lunch yesterday. He wasn't entirely happy about it, but he kept his promise. Last week, we agreed that if I got the timeline done by Friday, he would buy me lunch.

A person telling me I can't do a thing has always motivated me to do that thing. Sometimes I've met people see that as a positive way to get results. It isn't. I despise people who tell me I can't do something. The whole thing is based on negative emotions, so it's hard to get good out of it.

My parents used to do that all the time. They called it reverse psychology, and always said it as though they were really intelligent for putting one over on somebody. But then they'd get mad at you if you saw through what they were doing so their "reverse psychology" didn't work. Isn't that just dopey?

Parents invest years telling you to do as you're told. Then, when you do as you're told, it turns out they were trying to be all sophisticated and sneaky. So you get in trouble for doing what you were told to do. Insane.

The bright side is that I feel good for having gotten so much work done. Of course, I've been telling everyone at PADS and the folks at We Care about what I'm doing. They are hugely encouraging. The volunteers at the different PADS churches actually seem interested in what I'm doing. I mean, they ask me questions about their own situations, and how to connect with people they're worried about. That feels super good.

Denise, the lady who runs We Care, has spoken to me about the project a few times. She has good business sense, so I've also asked her some questions, and bounced ideas with her, about the Kickstarter and how to make the project attractive to business owners. It's a form of cause marketing, right? So it's like Jerry Lewis or the Cancer Society getting people interested in their cause.

It's the first time in my life that I'm looking at things that have happened, and actually doing something with them. I mean, some things have happened that are truly bad. Having parents who didn't want me springs to mind. But this is the first time that I'm looking at those things and deciding "What effect has that had? What do I want to do about that effect?"

I remember saying to Matthew Parks once that growing up without parents who loved me has left a hole in my psyche. Having loving parents is something other people had, and I didn't. Yes, that makes me different. No, there is no way to replace that experience. The fact is that I have to live with that gap. But that's no reason to believe I can't love a wife or child, and be a good husband and dad.

For a long time, I believed that's exactly what it meant. Even with Maria and the kids, I was unsure of myself and held back. I'm sorry for the pain that caused all of us. But I'm learning. I'm getting better. And writing this book is my tool for looking at, into, myself.

Dr. Glasser, the choice theory guy, says all we do is behave, and we choose our behavior. Okay. I think he's skimming over the reality of reflex, but I get the point. Dr. Maltz, the psycho-cybernetics guy, says the same sort of thing. He says we can decide who we want to be, and then we get there by trying and making correction as we go. John Maxwell makes the same point in his book *Failing Forward*. The faster we try, make mistakes, fix them, and learn, the faster we make progress toward our goal.

Day 136 – Tuesday, 26 Mar – Amazed, Grateful and Happy

I made lots of progress on putting a Facebook Page together for the book.

Then I went to talk with Denise at We Care about being able to use their telephone to do radio interviews. Jack Canfield did at least one radio interview every day to promote the *Chicken Soup* series, so I'm planning to follow his example.

"Hi, Denise, can I talk to you for a second?"

Denise is always upbeat and cheerful. "Sure, come on in. Have a seat.

"Let me just finish this and I'll be right with you."

I was nervous about asking for the favor, and enthusiastic about my project. My first words came out in a rush. "Denise, I have a favor to ask. I don't know how big it is, but it's big to me. And it's for my book project."

Naturally, as I had volunteered more regularly at We Care, I also talked with the staff and volunteers about what I was working on. Sometimes people got a little uncomfortable, but most reactions were positive and encouraging. Denise was one of the people who believed sharing my experiences might help a lot of people feel encouraged and understood.

"Sure, what is it?"

"Well, you probably know that promotion is the biggest part of making a book successful. My plan is to use material I have from Alex Carroll for getting radio interviews. The physical copy is still with Maria, but I have a digital copy, and most importantly it has his complete database of radio stations across the U.S."

I took a breath to see if she would say anything, but Denise waited patiently for me to get to the favor. "I have the book outlined, and have started writing. David Hancock at Morgan James Publishing has agreed to publish the book, and of course I have the books I've already published. The blogsite is put together for the book, and I'm working on social media. A Facebook page is put together, and I've connected Facebook, LinkedIn and Twitter to the blog.

"A Kickstarter campaign is planned, and I showed that to Ken Fields. He thinks it's very good. So now what I want to do is start doing radio interviews to develop traction for the book going into the Kickstarter. That's where the favor comes in.

Denise was smiling and listening. She hadn't asked questions, yet, although she had marked down a note or two.

"Doing radio interviews means needing access to a phone, and I know you have one in the resource room. But here's the thing... There are two ideal times for radio interviews. One is in the morning rush hour, and the other is afternoon rush hour.

"To get the morning rush hour means having access to the phone as early as five thirty in the morning."

Denise perked up with a gut reaction at that point. "Oh, that's early. I'm not sure we could get anyone to volunteer to be here that early. How often would you be doing interviews?"

"That's the thing... Once they get rolling, I'll be doing interviews every day.

"And I thought about having someone come in, that's where the big favor is. You see, what I'm wondering is whether you would consider letting me have a key to come in and use the phone on my own. That way nobody has to be here early."

"Oh, well... Yes, I think we could arrange that. You're already here volunteering most days.

"Let me think for a second."

Denise looked at her notes, and looked at something on her computer.

"How much of this do you have planned out?"

This always got me excited. I've always enjoyed

the planning process the most. "I have the book proposal; I needed that to get the publishing contract with Morgan James. That covers research for why the book is different, why I want to write, how it's going to be promoted, and what resources I need to write and promote the book.

"The Kickstarter is mostly planned. I have rewards and support levels worked out, the copy is outlined for the campaign page, and I have a script for the video. So I'm in good shape there.

"For the radio interviews, I have Alex Carroll's material as a guide, and I did lots of radio interviews for my book on social media. So I think I'm in good shape.

"There's still some work to do, but yes, it's pretty much planned and written down."

Denise was making notes while I talked, and nodding as we went. "Okay. That's good.

"And right now the one thing you need is access to a telephone?"

"Well, there are lots of things I could use, sure, but yes, a telephone is essential for doing the radio interviews."

"What about using a cell phone?"

"Well, that works in a pinch. I've done interviews via cell phone before, and it works, but cell phones have a tendency to break up. Sometimes they lose calls. The biggest thing is the battery. Sometimes interviews go for an hour. That's why a land line is really the best option."

Denise was deep in thought as she answered. "Right. That makes sense. And you need access to a phone early in the morning and during the afternoon. Hmmm…

"Yes, I'm sure we can help you with getting access to the phone. That's not a problem. But I have a little bit different idea."

Denise was smiling now. She had that look people sometimes get when they have a big idea, and it means doing something good for someone.

That's when she asked, "What if we help you get an apartment?"

It's a good thing I was sitting down. I think I might have fallen down if I weren't already sitting. It was like the blood rushed out of my body, and I was left weightless. I think my mouth might even have dropped open.

"Are you serious? Well, yea! I mean, of course! It would never have occurred to me to ask for something like that. Can you do that?"

Naturally there was some work to be done. Some forms needed filling, and I had to show them everything really was planned and written down. We got a copy of the publishing contract, and they helped with printing the book proposal, Kickstarter campaign, and promotional plan.

Of course, there was also the matter of having to find an apartment. Denise made it clear the rent had to be less than five hundred per month because that was the limit of their budget. Plus they could help with getting the phone and electricity connected.

The PADS program was ending in three weeks, so this was excellent timing. I was ecstatic.

Day 139 – Friday, 29 Mar – Excited, Satisfied, Drained

Material is filled in for the book outline all the way to the end of January. That feels very good, but it's also emotionally draining.

All the memories are so fresh. And it's more than just the memories of what is going on with Maria. The stories I plan to use as flashbacks are vivid and fresh, too. It makes sense, I guess, since these are the memories that most often play in my mind. That's why they have influence – because I replay and relive them so often.

Writing material in the outline is a lot like doing hard work. What I do each day makes me stronger for the next days' work. And when you've done a few days work, you're all worn out and need to rest.

I've been looking at apartments. Denise came by the library today to tell me about a one bedroom place above a restaurant. It feels so good to have somebody lending a hand and caring.

Day 140 – Saturday, 30 Mar – Happy, Challenged

The outline for *Getting Happy… when you wish you were dead* is done. I've connected emotions with each day and event.

It's a little funny, too. The first book I wrote took about six months to research, and the first draft was written in three days. This book has taken my whole life to prepare, and just the outline has taken ten days. I wonder how long it will take to write the whole book.

It feels good to have the outline done. It's like having a road map in place, and now I can look at doing additional work for the book.

Part of the reason why the Kickstarter and media plans are done is that I've been avoiding working on the book. It's hard, emotional work that often shows me in a bad light, and that deliberately stirs painful memories. Everybody, including me, is happy to see so much preparation and planning completed, but the truth is that it's all pointless without the manuscript. So I'm very happy at having this first, important step finished.

It's a good feeling to be challenged like this. Instead of just reliving memories, and letting them control me, I'm starting to sort what is my responsibility and what isn't. I feel like there should be Star Trek music playing, and someone standing behind me narrating with something like "Boldly going where this man has never gone before."

It's exciting and frightening at the same time.

There was more looking at apartments today. Some are just a phone call because they're taken, or the rent is too high. I went to see the apartment Denise told me about. It's above an Italian restaurant, and it's right downtown.

There are only twelve thousand people in town, so it's a little surprising to discover there are so many apartments. There are even two rooming houses in town.

Mike Lord told me an apartment just opened in his building. The apartments are above a funeral home so they're quiet, and the building is just two blocks away from the main downtown street. I'm going to look at it tomorrow.

Day 142 – Monday, 1 Apr – Vindicated, Productive and Happy

I left PADS this morning and went straight to Mike Lord's place. I want to be there when the owner of the funeral home arrives to talk with him about the apartment.

The entrance to his office is next to the entrance for the apartments. He's there when I go down to check just after nine am.

"Hi, good morning. May I talk to you about the apartment you have available?"

"By all means. Come in and have a seat."

He was a pleasant fellow. I guess you have to be friendly and easy to get along with in the funeral business.

"How did you hear about the apartment?"

"Mike Lord, one of your tenants, told me it's available."

"Oh, so then you know the building. You've seen Mike's apartment, have you?"

"Yes, I have. In fact, I was just visiting Mike

before coming to see you. It's a nice building."

"Yes, it is. And so you know, we like to keep it quiet. The funeral home is downstairs, so we can't have loud music or noises. If you live here, you have to keep in mind that this is funeral home first. It's a business."

That might come across as harsh, and he certainly was serious, but he wasn't being mean.

"Yes, sir. That's fine by me. I spent twenty years in construction. I've had my fill of loud noises."

We ended up not even going to see the apartment. Every apartment was a one bedroom, and since I had seen Mike's it didn't make sense to go look at an empty apartment. Instead, we talked about me, the book, and my plans, and him and his business.

It took a couple of trips to We Care to have the lease co-signed, get checks and deliver them, and show Denise the receipt. We finished with me having the keys, and the landlord asked if he could have the rest of the day to have the apartment cleaned.

He said I could come anytime tomorrow. The apartment would be all mine.

Day 143 – Tuesday, 2 Apr – Getting Very Happy

I got an apartment today!

It's down the hall from my friend, Mike. So I'll have somebody to talk to. That's cool. And it's a one bedroom apartment with a living room, dining room and kitchen. I don't have anything to put in it, but it's my apartment. That feels very good.

Squeezing the keys in my left hand… Standing in my living room… Looking at the "roof over my head," I turn toward the door of my new apartment. I close the door. Open it, and close it again. I lock it, and unlock it. It snaps firmly into place and has a satisfying click when opened. Lock it again, then unlock and open the door. I'm getting used to the idca of it being mine.

Turning left, I walk from the dining room into the kitchen just to look at it. Coming out of the kitchen, a right turn and short walk along the hall takes me to the bathroom on the right. Another step and I'm in the living room. The door to my bedroom is at my right hand. On the left, between the living and dining rooms is a walk-in closet so big it has two doors; one in the short hallway and the other in the dining room.

It's a small, elegant apartment in an old building. In fact, it's upstairs from the oldest funeral home in town. I'm glad it's a quiet building.

It has been quite a ride. My clients are gone. My marriage is over. But I have friends; people who care about me. *Getting Happy...when you wish you were dead* is getting written, and I hope it becomes a light for people. I feel like I've walked through hell and come out the other side. I'm getting happy and want to help other people do the same thing.

Acknowledgements

This story owes a huge debt of gratitude to my former wife for her choices. Her choices led to my being homeless in a foreign country, and living in an Out Of The Cold program. Those circumstances pushed me to look at my life and myself. This story could never have been written without her making her choices.

There is a long list of authors whose books helped me along the way. Dennis Greenberger, PhD and Christine A. Padesky, PhD who wrote *Mind Over Mood*. This book helped me to heal the damage done by so many years of being angry. Dr. Maxwell Maltz, Jack Canfield, John Maxwell, and Dale Carnegie for their motivation and instruction. Sarah Millican for *How To Be Champion*. Dr. Terry Lynch, Thomas Joiner, and Dr. William Glasser for their books on choice and the instruction they shared.

A very special note of thanks to Dan Kennedy. He is a mentor to talk to, a mentor to model, and a friend to cherish.

Last, but far from least, are the people who helped produce this book. My thanks to William Clark for editorial thoughts and suggestions. He helped me scrub the blame from the story.

Embedded Links

Links in the following pages may be affiliate inks or lead to pages that contain affiliate links. These are provided as an additional way for you to support the author in providing useful information to readers. Using the affiliate links provides a small commission to help support the author.

Thank you in advance for supporting Conrad Hall in helping readers everywhere move toward Getting Happy

Recommended Reading

Failing Forward, John Maxwell
(https://amzn.to/3sIFA1k)

How to be Champion, Sarah Millican
(https://amzn.to/3mml4T0)

How to Win Friends and Influence People, Dale Carnegie (https://amzn.to/389fZoZ)

Magnetic Marketing, Dan Kennedy
(https://amzn.to/3gelSWa)

Mind Over Mood, Dennis Greenberger, PhD and Christine Padesky, PhD
(https://amzn.to/3kkhAhn)

Psycho-Cybernetics, Dr. Maxwell Maltz
(https://amzn.to/3kjz6Cu)

Selfhood, Dr. Terry Lynch
(https://amzn.to/3yfjNjc)

The Success Principles, Jack Canfield
(https://amzn.to/3mc0S6j)

Warning: Psychiatry May Be Hazardous To Your Mental Health, Dr. William Glasser
(https://amzn.to/3gw8FZ7)

Reserve Story #2 in the *Getting Happy* Series
…Thinking About Divorce

In Your Hands Spring 2022

Divorce might be your best option. Then again, it's amazing how big the results can be from a small, steady effort.

It's no surprise so many marriages end in divorce when you consider most people put more effort into choosing a stereo or computer than they put into choosing their spouse. The common myth is that our warm and fuzzy feelings – what we call "being in love" – are supposed to be enough to sustain two people over decades of marriage.

Getting Happy …Thinking About Divorce is the story of three people who have faced and survived divorce. Divorce was the right choice for two of them. The third person faced divorce, discovered how to make the right effort, and saved the marriage.

Visit https://GettingHappyBook.com/divorce to reserve your copy of story #2 in the *Getting Happy* series.

Family Team Building

Making Sure the People We Love are Our Biggest Supporters

Blood is thicker than water, right? The love of a family is life's greatest blessing, but what happens when that love takes on a sinister tinge? How do we mend the ties that bind our family when they've gotten frayed by 21st Century distractions?

Fortunately, there's a simple answer to mending family ties. It's the same answer used by team builders the world over. You've used it yourself as a parent, a friend, or even coaching one of your kids' sports teams.

It's refereeing.

Coaching is a good thing. It helps people get better at something, right? Anyone can coach you and help you get better, but refereeing is different. Ever try telling your spouse they're wrong? How about trying to mend fences when your kids are feuding only to have them turn on you in fury?

The unfortunate truth is the average American family argues 217 times per year just over doing the dishes. A Capri-Sun survey of parents in the UK found they are arguing with their children (ages 2-12) six times per day. That's 2,184 arguments every year. It can be hard to build the family team when you feel overwhelmed by petty arguments.

That's when you need a referee. Someone outside the family to help sort right from wrong, and get your family back to using PEP (Personal Empowerment Practices).

Visit https://ceriohs.org/family-referee to find a referee for your family today.

Jack Canfield's
The Success Principles

Since its publication a decade ago, Jack Canfield's practical and inspiring guide has helped thousands of people transform themselves for success. Now, he has revised and updated his essential guidebook to reflect our changing times.

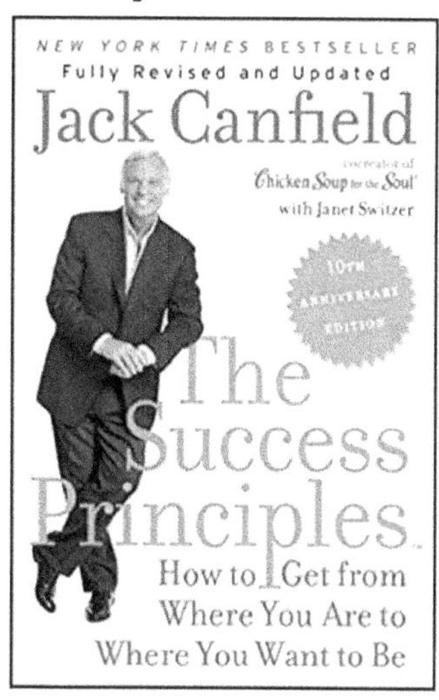

In *The Success Principles*™ (https://amzn.to/3mc0S6j), the co-creator of the phenomenal bestselling *Chicken Soup for the Soul*® series, helps you get from where you are to where you want to be, teaching you how to increase your confidence, tackle daily challenges, live with passion and purpose, and realize all your ambitions. Filled with memorable and inspiring stories of CEO's, world-class athletes, celebrities, and everyday people, it spells out the 64 timeless principles used by successful men and women throughout history — proven principles and strategies that can be adapted for your own life, whether you want to be the best salesperson in your company, become a leading architect, score top grades in school, lose weight, buy your dream home, make millions, or just get back in the job market.

Share Your Story

Have you had a life event where you started out unhappy and worked your way through to getting happy? Maybe starting university, or a new job, and being far from home was difficult. But you found your way to getting happy.

Maybe it was a negative event that rocked your world. Are you ready to share your story of being unhappy and making your way to getting happy?

The <u>Getting Happy</u> series uses true stories to show how people are affected by positive and negative life events. Then we build a workbook to go with the story. Your story can be a source of inspiration and motivation for other people. The workbook is for those who want a little extra direction for finding their way to getting happy.

And let's be clear: positive events can be just as stressful as negative. Having a baby is a wonderful experience, but those bundles of joy never come with an instruction manual. My wife and I found having a baby surprisingly intimidating. We were young, unprepared, and afraid to admit our shortcomings. I would have gladly read someone's story about how to work through that joyful event.

Everyone reacts to stress differently, yes? We even react to the same stress differently in different circumstances. We might be very upset and worried when our first child goes away to school. Then we handle it much better when each subsequent child leaves the nest. That is, until the last one leaves. Then we have a whole new problem because the nest is now empty.

Come share your story. Help someone be inspired and motivated.

Click here to share your story. Or visit https://GettingHappySeries.com/shareyourstory. That's all lowercase letters for "shareyourstory" and type it with no spaces.

Invite Conrad Hall to Your Next Event

Known for his Cranium Ex Rectum™ approach, Conrad regularly brings audiences to their feet with applause and cheers. He speaks on a wide array of topics from self-image and how to build it to Robust Parenting to Showing Up For Success.

Reach out to book Conrad for your next event, show, or podcast. Or tap him for a soundbite on his expertise.

1.647.278.0188
Conrad@CERIOHS.org

About the Author

Little children and animals have always loved me. Horses no one else could handle were quiet for me. Dogs and cats that never like anyone get cozy with me. And children who won't go to anyone except Mom or Grandma fall asleep on my shoulder. It's a strange way to start a bio, but these are important things to remember as you read about me.

I was born the third child in a family with two children, and my parents made sure I knew my place. It's a hard thing to grow up in a family that doesn't want you. There is something in all of us that is supposed to be nurtured by the love of Mom and Dad. I have been temporarily blinded twice in my life because of accidents. My experience is it's easier to deal with blindness than it is to grow without the essential emotional nutrition of parental love.

When I asked to live with Aunt Geri and Uncle Harold, the answer was telling. After I had the audacity to catch her in repeated lies, my mother rather hotly explained saying "She raised Fran's kids and Anne's kids. I'll be damned if she's going to raise one of mine."

When I was ten, I once asked for help sorting money to pay for my four paper routes. My mother's answer was "We told you not to take those paper routes. So now you can deal with them on your own."

Growing up rejected by my parents made me believe everyone would feel the same way toward me. After all, who is going to love you when your parents don't, right? It made me a hard person to understand, and I grew into a hard man. For a big part of my life, I lived by the motto "Yea though I walk through the valley of death, I shall fear no evil, for I am the meanest S.O.B. in the valley."

I have lived on both sides of the law with considerable skills as a thief and as a drug dealer. I've also served in the military, run a carpentry business, been married, and am a father.

Yet, no matter what I was doing, I was never inclined to tolerate stupidity. I have no trouble with someone who has genuine difficulty learning something. We all need a little help with new concepts, right? But I have never had patience for people being willfully stupid.

It was routine for people to be surprised, even shocked, when their courteous co-worker, polite contractor, or considerate drug dealer was suddenly calling them out for their stupidity.

Of course, my stupidity was combining the expectation of rejection with every subsequent rejection and thinking it all proved my parents were right; I'm not worth loving. After all, our society is built upon premises such as parents loving their children, and the reality of parents imparting their beliefs to their children.

No one should be surprised when unloved children grow into adults who behave in ways that prove their parents right. Everyone loves the result when we get a professional athlete, successful entrepreneur, or effective activist. But we turn around and blame the person who is anti-social, cruel, or rude. Yet, they might all be striving to meet parental expectations.

To my credit, I started breaking free of parental expectations around age 19. I had always been rebellious, but childhood and teenage rebellion are different from consciously assessing what you're doing, and your reasons for doing it.

My reasons have led to great choices that resulted in employment success, achieving wealth as a business owner, a wide base of learning through continuing education and reading, and some wonderfully, temporarily, happy relationships.

My choices have also managed to lead to bankruptcy three times (once instigated by my father), being homeless five times (twice by deliberate choice), spending time in jail, and living through more than fifty years without forming a single long-lasting relationship. Even the children to whom I was a father are no longer part of my life.

One child is mine by blood. Another three came into my life by marriage.

At this point, you might be thinking I am quite the jerk. You're right to think so. I have been a consummate jerk in my lifetime, and I have no fear of offending people by speaking the truth. Even my good, positive choices ended up marred by self-sabotage.

It took a lot of learning, and a long time, to realise two things:

1. All we have is the reality in front of us; and,

2. A lot of people are desperate to avoid reality

The only thing I can control is how I choose to behave. If you doubt that truth, just ask any parent what it's like to "control" an over-tired, cranky toddler. And you can see the truth of it in everyday life by watching people who accept wage-slavery and then complain about having no control.

I have invested an incredible amount of time listening to business owners, parents, and young adults as they defend their stupid choices, and, more importantly, as they change course for better choices. And the intellectual spectrum covers everyone from doctors and tradesmen, to teachers, PhD students, and labourers. It is stunning to see how deeply the desire to be accepted as right, in the face of all opposition and contradiction, permeates our society. Even more amazing is seeing the relief that washes through someone when they succeed in fixing a mistake. Bill is a great example.

Bill owns a truck repair shop. When his employees asked for a raise, he had the habit of crying poverty by telling them it had been years since he had a paycheque from the business. While this was true, it was far from the truth. I managed to bring Bill back to reality by telling him precisely that. Yes, it had been years since his last paycheque, but he had arranged it to his benefit. In a perfectly legal accounting move, Bill arranged it so his investment into the business over the years was a loan. So yes, he was getting paid, and he had arranged it so the payments were tax free because the business was repaying the loan.

Things got a lot smoother between Bill and his employees when he finally confessed this truth and started passing along some of the business' success in the form of raises.

When you add up all the hours of listening and coaching, it turns out to be years and years of experience. Parents concerned about their children. Children angry with their parents. Business owners confused about leadership and customer relations. The experiences of listening, accepting, being honest and consistent, caring and encouraging, smoothed the rougher edges left from an angry, abused, and rebellious young man.

Those experiences, and a life-altering divorce, led me to pull back, look honestly at myself, and strip away my private lies and pretentions.

My life motto today is simply Cranium Ex Rectum™.

Yes, pull your head out of your arse and face the reality in front of you instead of what you wish were in front of you. You can tell when people get it because they laugh. You can tell people who need a healthy dose of Cranium Ex Rectum™ because they get upset and offended.

The whole point of the phrase Cranium Ex Rectum™ is to play on the pretentions of erudition (real or imagined). It's a phrase that sounds lofty in Latin that turns out to be simple, even crass, advice. Stop kidding yourself. Stop lying to yourself and others. Pull your head out of your arse.

My adult life – all the good and all the bad – is the direct result of choices I've made. Knowing that is what moved me to choose being an author. I learned a lot about myself, making and fixing mistakes, and how other people behave from the choices I've made. The best way to share that learning is writing it down, yes?

I've already written seven books on marketing. Two of those are international bestsellers. It turns out running your own business from newspaper routes to residential renovations, and doing all the promotion and customer relations, is a great start for an education on marketing. The bigger education, by far, has been learning to understand myself and the people around me.

Have you ever heard the phrase "When you find yourself in a hole, put down the shovel?" Well, it's fair to say I started life in a hole of negative self-image. I made that hole wider and deeper by holding onto rage and being cruel to people around me. Eventually, I put down the shovel, fashioned stairs to leave that hole, and built a strong, positive self-image. Was it all roses and honey? No. And I make no claim to having a perfect life now- nor am I anywhere near being a perfect man. There are still lots of people who think I'm a jerk.

And make no mistake, the hole is still there. There is nothing that can replace love and support that was never present. However, real effort can transform a crappy, dingy crawl space into a warm, light-filled, friendly, finished basement.

I'm just a man who has learned to stand on his own two feet, makes the best choices he can, and accepts responsibility for those choices. I have always been a man loved by little children and animals.